TABLE OF CONTENTS

ACRONYMS

ADP	Army Doctrine Publication
ADRP	Army Doctrine Reference Publication
AFDD	Air Force Doctrine Document
ATP	Army Techniques Publication
ATTP	Army Tactics, Techniques, and Procedures
CASEVAC	Casualty Evacuation
CENTCOM	United States Central Command
CMO	Civil-Military Operations
CMRT	Combined Medical Relief Team
CSF	Combined Support Force
DoD	U.S. Department of Defense
DODI	Department of Defense Instruction
EMEDS	Expeditionary Medical Support
EXTAC	Experimental Tactic
FDR	Foreign Disaster Relief
FHA	Foreign Humanitarian Assistance
FM	Field Manual
FSO	Full Spectrum Operations
HA	Humanitarian Assistance
HADR	Humanitarian Assistance Disaster Relief
IGO	Inter-Governmental Organization
JP	Joint Publication
JTF	Joint Task Force
MASH	Mobile Army Surgical Hospital
MEDEVAC	Medical Evacuation
MEDCAP	Medical Civil Action Program

MHS	Military Health Systems
NATO	North Atlantic Treaty Organization
NGO	Non-Governmental Organization
OOTW	Operations Other Than War
OFDA	Office of Disaster Assistance
OHDACA	Overseas Humanitarian, Disaster, and Civic Aid
PACOM	United States Pacific Command
TACMEMO	Tactical Memorandum
TM	Technical Manual
UN	United Nations
UNOSOM	United Nations Operation in Somalia
USAID	United States Agency for International Development
USNS	United States Naval Ship
USS	United States Ship
VTOL	Vertical Take-off and Landing

ILLUSTRATIONS

TABLES

INTRODUCTION

The United States Military's projection of national power is not limited to its ability to fight and win the nation's wars. The military's greatest utility lies within the strategic message that it transmits throughout the world by virtue of its presence.[1] As the *National Security Strategy* has outlined, our ability to "promote dignity by meeting human needs" within the humanitarian context is a symbol of national strength, pride, and values.[2] This message has been transmitted through a spectrum of actions that have come to be known as foreign humanitarian assistance (FHA) operations.[3] This monograph will discuss foreign disaster relief (FDR) within FHA operations.[4] In this document, FDR may be described as the emergency measures used to address disaster related impediments towards the achievement of social well-being.[5]

Decisive FDR operations often do not rely on weapons systems, but on a vast array of sustainment assets.[6] At a basic interpretation, military sustainment assets are designed to quickly meet the diverse needs of a massive population that is trying to survive under austere conditions.[7]

---

[1] The investment of military force in the global good is the essence of what Joseph Nye has labeled as "Smart Power".

[2] The White House, *National Security Strategy* (Washington, D.C.: White House, 2010), 39.

[3] Within joint doctrine, foreign humanitarian assistance is one of five stability operations functions (JP 3-07).

[4] U.S. Department of Defense, *Department of Defense Support to Foreign Disaster Relief*, GTA 90-01-030 (Washington D.C.: Government Printing Office, 2011), ix.

[5] In U.S. Army doctrine (ADRP 3-07), this encompasses stability actions that fall under Department of State "Primary Stability Tasks," DoD "Joint Stability Functions," and Army "Stability Sectors."

[6] U.S. Department of Defense, *Foreign Humanitarian Assistance,* JP 3-29 (Washington, D.C.: Government Printing Office, 2009), vii-xi.

[7] U.S. Department of the Army, *Sustainment,* ADP 4-0 (Washington, D.C.: Government

Training, equipment, and organization often afford the Department of Defense (DoD) the ability to provide FDR ahead of the non-governmental, inter-governmental (NGO-IGO), and inter-agency community within a "Gap of Pain" (as depicted by #7 in Figure 1).[8] This capability has made the Department of Defense (DoD) an obvious stakeholder in the execution of FDR.[9] While always tragic, disasters provide a venue for the American government to demonstrate its national values of care and compassion.[10]

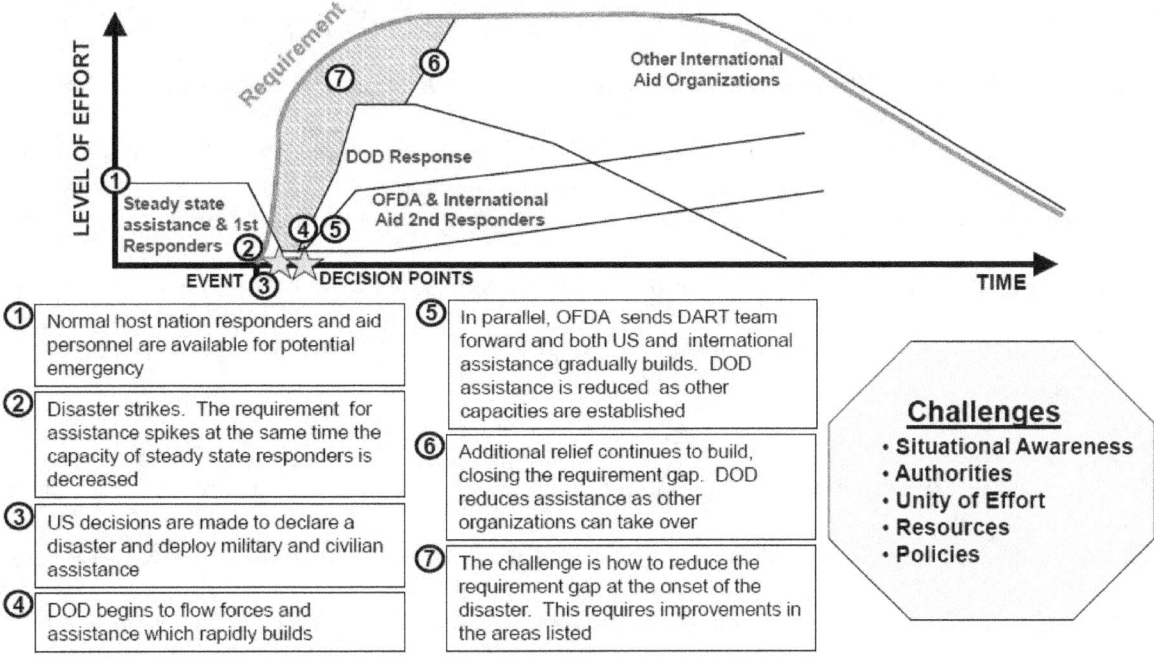

Figure 1: "The Gap of Pain" that this monograph aims to address.[11]

Printing Office, 2012), 3-4.

[8]Sharon Wiharta et al., *The Effectiveness of Foreign Military Assets in Natural Disaster Response* (Solna, Sweden, The Stockholm International Peace Research Institute, 2008), 9.

[9]U.S. Department of the Army, *Sustainment,* ADP 4-0 (Washington, D.C.: Government Printing Office, 2012), 14.

[10]The National Research Council, *The U.S. Government Foreign Disaster Assistance Program* (Washington, D.C.: National Academy of Sciences, 1978), 15.

[11]Joint Center for Operational Analysis, "Operation Unified Response: Haiti Earthquake

Army doctrine provides a three-phased framework for stability operations: initial response phase, transformation phase, and fostering sustainability phase. Among the most critical requirements in the initial response phase of a disaster is the provision of medical care to those who are sick or wounded.[12] This monograph will often refer to the initial response as the "emergency phase" in order to emphasize the perishability of the victims. The DoD's vast medical resources have the capacity to reduce civilian human suffering and assist governments in reestablishing a sense of stability. In order to achieve this, the appropriate assets must to be ready for rapid employment with the capabilities relevant to the FDR operational approach. These capabilities must be responsive to the changing environmental conditions and reliably restore the social well-being of the affected population to an acceptable level.[13] Although the U.S. military has a history of providing medical aid following disasters throughout the world, the quantity and quality of this type of foreign humanitarian relief has risen precipitously since the end of the Cold War.[14]

From the 1992 famine relief in Somalia to the 2010 Haitian earthquake relief effort, there appears to be an evolution towards connecting a combatant commander's military medical means to the desired strategic message within the international community. The DoD has improved the efficacy of health service support to combatant commanders within emergent foreign humanitarian assistance operations by training, reorganizing and equipping rapidly employable

---

Response" (after action review presentation, Norfolk, VA, May 15, 2010).

[12]U.S. Department of the Army, *Stability,* ADP 3-07 (Washington, D.C.: Government Printing Office, 2012), 1-12 to 1-13.

[13]U.S. Department of the Army, *Army Health System,* FM 4-02 (Washington, D.C.: Government Printing Office, 2013) 2-2 to 2-5.

[14]Sharon Wiharta et al., *The Effectiveness of Foreign Military Assets in Natural Disaster Response* (Solna, Sweden: The Stockholm International Peace Research Institute, 2008), 9.

military health systems (MHS). This monograph establishes a framework to measure that improvement. By assessing the suitability of MHS within FDR, one may begin to examine the mechanisms that were successful at reducing global human suffering and identify opportunities for exploitation in the DoD's global health engagement strategy.

Methodology and Terminology

This monograph will examine the efficacy of MHS in FDR operations in recent history. It seeks to determine whether DoD health systems have evolved as effective instruments to fill the gap of pain within the initial phase of a disaster. By developing an understanding of MHS' emerging role within FDR, we can critically analyze and creatively develop solutions towards the effective training, organization, and equipping of the joint-force. This study will accomplish this by reviewing current and historical joint and service component oriented doctrine and policy. This review will represent the military's body of knowledge regarding its own utility within FDR environments throughout recent history. The monograph will then examine four case studies involving the employment of MHS, all of which have taken place within the last 20 years. These case studies will illustrate how effectively the joint-force applied its body of knowledge. The case studies examined include Operation Restore Hope (Somalia-1992 through 1993), Operation Unified Assistance (Indonesia-2004), Operation Lifeline (Pakistan-2005), and Operation Unified Response (Haiti-2010). Although this monograph assesses the DoD's joint response, the technical terminology that it utilizes will generally remain consistent with U.S. Army doctrine.[15]

---

[15]One notable exception to this is the use of "foreign disaster relief" (FDR) as outlined in the preface to the *Department of Defense Support to Foreign Disaster Relief* opposed to "foreign humanitarian assistance (FHA) as outlined in the Army Doctrinal Reference Publication (ADRP) titled *Stability*.

Within these case studies, this monograph will highlight the employment of the Army's health service support warfighting function.[16] It consists of medical evacuation, hospitalization, and medical logistics activities. [17] "Medical evacuation" (MEDEVAC) is the system of sustaining a patient during transport by land, air, or sea to a level of medical care that provides the level of specialty care that a patient requires. MEDEVAC is not to be confused with "casualty evacuation" (CASEVAC), which implies the transportation of casualties without benefit of en-route medical care.[18] Throughout this monograph, the term "evacuation" will be used to capture both. "Hospitalization" refers to the ability to conduct casualty care tasks consistent with a Role III medical treatment facility. These tasks include emergency care, forward resuscitative surgery, laboratory services, radiological services, blood services, pharmacy support, and specialty care.[19] "Medical logistics" includes the procurement and distribution of medical supplies, repair and maintenance of medical materiel, production and distribution of medical gases, blood management, and medical waste management.[20] This monograph will also frame the movement of medical personnel within the context of medical logistics.

The medical functions described will be qualitatively evaluated using three principles of the Army's Health Systems. They are proximity, flexibility, and continuity. "Proximity" addresses a medical function's ability to provide support to a patient at the right time in order

---

[16]U.S. Department of the Army, *Army Health System,* FM 4-02 (Washington, D.C.: Government Printing Office, 2013) 7-1.

[17]Ibid., 1-5 to 1-7.

[18]U.S. Department of the Army, *Medical Evacuation,* FM 4-02.2 (Washington, D.C.: Government Printing Office, 2011) 1-7.

[19]U.S. Department of the Army, *Army Health System,* FM 4-02 (Washington D.C.: Government Printing Office, 2013), 7-3 to 7-5.

[20]Ibid., 9-1.

keep morbidity and mortality to a minimum. "Flexibility" addresses a medical function's ability to conform to the needs of the population as the operating environment changes. "Continuity" refers to the ability to transition a patient through phases of care. In the context of a FDR operation, continuity will pertain to the MHS' ability to coordinate its medical activities with adjacent relief organizations as well as the transition of patient care to the host nation's organic medical system.[21]

Foreign Disaster Relief has evolved within military doctrine and policy; the lexicon associated with it has evolved, as well. Nuanced activities such as Foreign Humanitarian Assistance (FHA), Foreign Disaster Assistance (FDA), and Humanitarian Assistance and Disaster Relief (HADR) are often used interchangeably with FDR throughout doctrine, policy, and literature.[22] It is also important to consider that FDR is sometimes clustered with the broader operational terms Humanitarian Assistance (HA) operations, Civil-Military Operations (CMO), Support to Civil Authorities, Stability Operations, Support Operations, Operations Other Than War (OOTW), and Full Spectrum Operations (FSO). As these doctrinal terms are referenced, it may be assumed by the reader that FDR lies within those classifications.

Literature Review

There are two epochs concerning FDR operations within U.S. military doctrine. The first is doctrine that was written before and during the Cold War. The earliest recorded act of U.S. Government involvement in FDR occurred in March of 1812 when Congress passed legislation to aid earthquake victims in Venezuela. This did not occur without controversy however and

---

[21]U.S. Department of the Army, *Army Health System,* FM 4-02 (Washington D.C.: Government Printing Office, 2013), 1-5 to 1-7.

[22]U.S. Department of Defense, *Department of Defense Support to Foreign Disaster Relief: Handbook for JTF Commanders and Below,* GTA 90-01-030 (Washington, D.C.: Government Printing Office, 2011), 1-1.

Congress frequently voted against subsequent FDR legislation. Despite this, Congress did authorize U.S. Navy vessels to transport privately donated relief supplies to stricken countries after the 1812 incident.[23] U.S. military forces conducted direct FDR at least as early as 1908 during this period when the Great White Fleet diverted to Messina, Sicily to assist in earthquake and tsunami relief.[24] These haphazard efforts provided strategic messaging, but depended on informal methods to understand needs. It was not until 1965 that the fledgling U.S. Agency for International Development Office of Foreign Disaster Assistance (USAID-OFDA) reluctantly requested that the DoD dispatch a military disaster assessment team to El Salvador following an earthquake.[25]

While these examples illustrate a utility for U.S. military forces in FDR prior to the 1990s, medical preparedness was not emphasized in either policy or doctrine. From 1942 to 1970, U.S. Army medical doctrine scarcely mentioned the roles or considerations that medics must take in regards to civilians.[26] The United States' FDR program was not formally organized until 1964.[27] DoD policy formalized that FDR was primarily the Department of State's realm

---

[23]The National Research Council, *The U.S. Government Foreign Disaster Assistance Program* (Washington, D.C.: National Academy of Sciences, 1978), 7.

[24]Bruce Ellman, "Waves of Hope: The U.S. Navy's Response to the Tsunami in Northern Indonesia" (monograph, Naval War College, 2007), 5.

[25]The National Research Council, *The U.S. Government Foreign Disaster Assistance Program* (Washington, D.C.: National Academy of Sciences, 1978), 18.

[26]This is based on a review of the Army's foundational medical doctrine commonly known as FM 8-10 from 1942 to 1970. The doctrine throughout this period uses the term "disaster" occasionally, however it is in the context of its effects on combat forces or a nuclear attack involving civilians. Joint medical doctrine had not come into existence at this moment.

[27]The National Research Council, *The U.S. Government Foreign Disaster Assistance Program* (Washington D.C.: National Academy of Sciences, 1978) 9.

that year in DoD Directive 5100.46.[28] It was not until 1967 that a pilot program was organized to allow USAID-OFDA to stockpile disaster relief supplies on DoD facilities around the world.[29] In 1970, Field Manual (FM) 8-10, *Medical Support Theater of Operations* was published. While this document does not directly address disasters, it does address Army medic's role in stability operations and the usefulness of medical civic actions.[30] In operational terms, the U.S. Army's capstone doctrine titled *Operations* (FM 100-5) did not emphasize a role for Army forces prior to the end of the Cold War.[31]

President George H.W. Bush declared the end of the Cold War on January 28, 1992.[32] The newly established global order ushered in a second epoch in U.S. military FDR policy and doctrine.[33] In June of 1993, the fourth major revision of FM 100-5 was published.[34] The inclusion of a chapter on operations other than war indicated an anomaly within normal military science.[35] While the participation in operations that did not equate to war was nothing new to the

---

[28]U.S. Department of Defense, *Responsibility for Foreign Disaster Relief Operations*, Department of Defense Directive 5100.46 (Washington, D.C., 1964), 2.

[29]The National Research Council, *The U.S. Government Foreign Disaster Assistance Program* (Washington D.C.: National Academy of Sciences, 1978), 18.

[30]U.S. Department of the Army, *Medical Support Theater of Operations*, FM 8-10 (Washington D.C.: Government Printing Office, 1970).

[31]This is the summation of a review of the U.S. Army's capstone operating doctrine, *Operations* (FM 100-5) from 1968 to 1986.

[32] Sharon Hanes and Richard Hanes, *Cold War Primary Sources* (Farmington Hills, MI: UXL, 2004), 319-323.

[33]Lois M. Davis et al. *Army Medical Support for Peace Operations and Humanitarian Assistance* (Santa Monica, CA: RAND Corporation, 1996), 1.

[34]U.S. Department of the Army, *Operations,* FM 100-5 (Washington, D.C.: Government Printing Office, 1993), sec. 13-5.

[35]Thomas S. Kuhn, *The Structure of Scientific Revolutions,* 3rd. ed. (Chicago: The University of Chicago Press, 1996), 52.

military, 1993's FM 100-5 stresses 13 activities within military operations other than war. The manual took the additional unprecedented step of clarifying a distinction between "Support to Domestic Civil Authorities" and "Humanitarian Assistance and Disaster Relief" activities.[36]

Acceptance of a change to the military's operating environment cascaded after the publication of 1993's FM 100-5. In September of that same year, the first version of Joint Publication (JP) 3-0 *Doctrine for Joint Operations* was published. This document reiterated FM 100-5's assertions on military operations other than war.[37] In 1994, the Army expanded on its humanitarian body of knowledge by publishing FM 100-23-1 *Multiservice Procedures for Humanitarian Assistance*. While not exclusively dedicated to FDR operations, it is laden with vignettes from Somalia's Operation Restore Hope.[38] It minimizes the relevance of the health services by promoting the assumption that MHS will not provide direct care to civilian patients unless they are injured by coalition actions.[39] That same year the Amy Medical Department published FM 8-55 "Planning for Health Service Support." Although this publication acknowledges FM 100-5's assertion of a military role in humanitarian activities, most of the medical contribution is encapsulated under medical civil action programs (MEDCAP). These programs are humanitarian in nature and may take place in a FDR environment, however they are commonly conducted under stable conditions as an effort to influence populations in

---

[36]U.S. Department of the Army, *Operations,* FM 100-5 (Washington, D.C.: Government Printing Office, 1993), Chapter 13.

[37]U.S. Department of Defense, *Doctrine for Joint Operations,* JP 3-0 (Washington, D.C.: Government Printing Office, 1993), Chapter 5.

[38]U.S. Department of Defense, *Multiservice Procedures for Humanitarian Assistance Operations,* FM 100-23-1 (Washington, D.C.: Government Printing Office, 1994).

[39]William A. Mosier and Walter H. Orthner, "Military Medical Support for Humanitarian Assistance and Disaster Relief: Lessons Learned From the Pakistan Earthquake Relief Effort," *Joint Center for Operational Analysis* 9, no. 2 (June 2007): 4.

underdeveloped communities.[40] That same year, the Department of Defense instituted the

Overseas Humanitarian, Disaster, and Civic Aid (OHDACA) allocations into defense

appropriations as a funding source for combatant commanders to influence international disaster

related contingencies.[41]

Joint and service component FDR health service doctrine grew exponentially throughout

the mid-1990s. In 1995, JP 3-07 *Joint Doctrine for Military Operations Other Than War* was

published. This manual explicitly addresses the DoD's role in FDR activities.[42] That same year,

MHS's humanitarian contribution to operations other than war was further clarified in JP 4-02

Doctrine for Health Service Support in Joint Operations.[43] The U.S. Navy published a detailed

technical manual as well, titled *Humanitarian Assistance/Disaster Relief Operations Planning* or

Technical Manual (TM) 3-07.6-05.[44] A respectable 80-page document in its own right, the Navy

followed up 3-07.6-05 the following year by circulating the 200-page EXTAC 1011 titled *Naval*

Humanitarian Assistance Missions throughout North Atlantic Treaty Organization (NATO)

navies. This document dedicates a 22-page annex towards the detailed application of health

services under HADR conditions. Of note, it explores in depth the challenges of domain interface

---

[40]U.S. Department of the Army, *Planning for Health Service Support,* FM 8-55 (Washington, D.C.: Government Printing Office, 1994).

[41]U.S. Department of Defense, "Fiscal Year 2013 Budget Estimates, Defense Security Cooperation Agency, February 2013." http://comptroller.defense.gov/defbudget/fy2013/budget_justification/pdfs/01_Operation_and_M aintenance/O_M_VOL_1_PARTS/O_M_VOL_1_BASE_PARTS/OHDACA_OP-5.pdf (accessed August 30, 2013).

[42]U.S. Department of Defense, *Joint Doctrine for Military Operations Other Than War,* JP 3-07 (Washington, D.C.: Government Printing Office, 1995), III-4, sec g.

[43]U.S. Department of Defense, *Doctrine for Health Service Support in Joint Operations,* JP 4-02 (Washington, D.C.: Government Printing Office, 1995).

[44]U.S. Department of the Navy, *Humanitarian Assistance/Disaster Relief Operations Planning,* TM 3-07.6-05 (Washington, D.C.: Government Printing Office, 1996), 12.

10

concerning the treatment, evacuation, and medical logistics system across land, sea, and air.[45]

Also in 1996, the U.S. Air Force issued Air Force Doctrine Document (AFDD) 2-3. While this 57-page document is dedicated solely to operations other than war, it affords one paragraph to foreign humanitarian assistance of every type.[46]

Throughout the remainder of the1990s, the Army and Air Force published updates to their medical doctrine. First came the release of JP 4-02.2 *Joint Tactics, Techniques, and Procedures for Patient Movement in Joint Operations*. This 1996 publication outlines the MHS' evacuation system.[47] Although this publication maintains a general focus at operations other than war, it facilitated unity in effort within FDR aeromedical evacuation planning by designating the U.S. Army as the lead agency to conduct shore-to-ship and ship-to-shore medical transport operations.[48] A year later, the Army issued a field manual titled *Combat Health Support in Stability Operations and Support Operations*. While the manual translates much of JP 3-07 into Army parlance, the manual's significance lies within its partition of FDR from a stability operation to a support operation in which civilians are likely to be the primary recipient of military health services.[49] In 1999, the U.S. Air Force published AFDD 2-4.2 *Health Services*. At 46 pages, the doctrine does little more than acknowledge that the U.S. Air Force has the

---

[45]U.S. Department of the Navy, *Naval Humanitarian Assistance Missions,* EXTAC 1011 (Washington, D.C.: Government Printing Office, 2005).

[46]U.S. Department of the Air Force, *Operations Other Than War,* Air Force Doctrine Document 2-3 (Washington, D.C.: Government Printing Office, 1996), 12.

[47]U.S. Department of Defense, *Doctrine for Health Service Support in Joint Operations,* JP 4-02 (Washington, D.C.: Government Printing Office, 1994).

[48]Darrel Whitcomb, *Call Sign-Dustoff: A History of U.S. Army Aeromedical Evacuation from Conception to Katrina* (Fort Detrick, MD: Office of the Surgeon General, 2011), 205.

[49]U.S. Department of the Army, *Combat Health Support in Stability Operations and Support Operations,* FM 8-42 (Washington, D.C.: Government Printing Office, 1997) 1-1.

capability to deploy medical assets for humanitarian purposes. It does not differentiate disaster relief from any other type of humanitarian mission as do joint and sister service publications from this period.[50]

The new millennium brought increasing levels of specificity to service doctrine regarding FDR. The Army's newest capstone doctrine codified the distinction between stability and support operations throughout the operational force.[51] The 2000 version of *Operations* goes much further in detail than its predecessor towards addressing the types of support operations and offers guidance to operational commanders for the employment of combat service support assets in FDR.[52] In 2001, JP 3-07.6 *Joint Tactics, Techniques, and Procedures for Foreign Humanitarian Assistance* replaced FM 100-23-1.[53] Major updates to this publication include an elaboration of the relationship between DoD, USAID-OFDA, and the ambassador. It goes on to sanction the combatant commander's ability to deploy humanitarian assistance survey teams (HAST), establishes health service support guidelines, identifies funding procedures, and emphasizes the importance of training for humanitarian operations during joint exercises.[54] The same year an update was published to JP 4-02 *Doctrine for Health Service Support in Joint*

---

[50]U.S. Department of the Air Force, *Health Services,* Air Force Doctrine Document 2-4.2 (Washington, D.C.: Government Printing Office, 1999).

[51]*Operations* changed at this time from FM 100-5 to FM 3-0 to synchronize with the joint publication system.

[52]U.S. Department of the Army, *Operations,* FM 3-0 (Washington D.C.: Government Printing Office, 2000) Chapter 10.

[53]This period saw the emergence of mainstream joint publications (JP). This was a departure from the services practice of providing operating concepts that were to be applied across the joint force. Several of the Army's field manuals were migrated to JPs during this period.

[54]U.S. Department of Defense, *Joint Tactics, Techniques, and Procedures for Foreign Humanitarian Assistance,* JP 3-07.6 (Washington, D.C.: Government Printing Office, 2001), vii-xi.

Operations. The publication designates disaster planning as a priority for the joint force surgeon although it generally offers less detail than its predecessor regarding FDR by deferring the reader to JP 3-07.[55] Two years later, the U.S. Army Medical Department released FM 4-02 *Force Health Protection in a Global Environment* as an update to its foundational doctrine.[56] This doctrine's significance to FDR lies within its categorization of the Army Medical Department into ten functional areas that may be arrayed to provide a flexible response to a disaster area.[57]

Almost all of the joint force's FDR doctrine that is used today was assembled after the 2004 tsunami in Southeast Asia. This period heralded a maturation of MHS into the FDR arena. This may have been a direct result of the DoD's policy shift towards emphasizing stability operations in 2005.[58] That year, the Naval Warfare Development Command also released TACMEMO 3-07.6-05. This document harvested many of the lessons learned from the previous year's tsunami response translates them into an 80-page FDR guide for naval commanders at every echelon from the strike group to ship. One chapter is dedicated solely to the application of health service support.[59] In 2009, JP 3-29 *Foreign Humanitarian Assistance* replaced JP 3-07.6 and incorporated an entire annex towards health services.[60] Several of the lessons learned cite the

[55]U.S. Department of Defense, *Doctrine for Health Service Support in Joint Operations,* JP 4-02 (Washington, D.C.: Government Printing Office, 2001).

[56]Capstone Army medical doctrine changed at this time from FM 8-10 to FM 4-02 to synchronize with the joint publication system.

[57]U.S. Department of the Army, *Force Health Protection in a Global Environment,* FM 4-02 (Washington, D.C.: Government Printing Office, 2003), Chapter 5.

[58]U.S. Department of Defense, *Stability Operations,* Department of Defense Directive 3000.05 (Washington, D.C., 2005), 2-4.

[59]U.S. Department of the Navy, *Humanitarian Assistance/Disaster Relief Operations Planning,* NWDC TACMEMO 3-07.6-05 (Washington, D.C.: Government Printing Office, 2005), Chapter 8.

[60]Department of Defense, *Foreign Humanitarian Assistance,* JP 3-29 (Washington, D.C.:

2005 Pakistan earthquake response as examples.[61] Strategic defense policy was updated that year as well with the publication of DODI 3000.5, which reasserted the DoD's commitment to maintain capacity to respond to humanitarian crisis.[62] A year later, the DoD policy elevated military medical support to stability operations to the same priority as combat operations.[63]

Army Tactics, Technics, and Procedures (ATTP) 4-02 superseded FM 4-02 in 2011 to become the Medical Department's base operating doctrine.[64] Substantial improvement the Army Medical Department's ability to quickly and flexibly deploy through capability based modules (See figure 2).[65] The document also enables continuity by dedicating a nine-page annex towards generating global medical intelligence that may forecast requirements in a FDR response.[66] That same year, the DoD released a 314-page handbook for Joint Task Force (JTF) commanders titled "Department of Defense Support to Foreign Disaster Relief." This comprehensive handbook guides joint task force commanders through disaster types, roles, responses, and resources available. Reliance on MHS is heavily emphasized.[67]

Government Printing Office, 2009), IV-24.

[61]Department of Defense, *Foreign Humanitarian Assistance,* JP 3-29 (Washington, D.C.: Government Printing Office, 2009), Appendix E.

[62]U.S. Department of Defense, *Stability Operations*, Department of Defense Instruction 3000.05 (Washington, D.C., 2009), 2.

[63]U.S. Department of Defense, *Military Health Support for Stability Operations*, Department of Defense Instruction 6000.16 (Washington, D.C., 2010), 1.

[64]In 2011, the Army Combined Arms Doctrine Directorate adopted the "Doctrine 2015" initiative. This program replaced several FMs with ATTPs and Army Technical Publications (ATPs).

[65]U.S. Department of the Army, *Army Health System,* ATTP 4-02 (Washington, D.C.: Government Printing Office, 2011), 1-4.

[66]Ibid., Annex A.

[67]U.S. Department of Defense, *Department of Defense Support to Foreign Disaster*

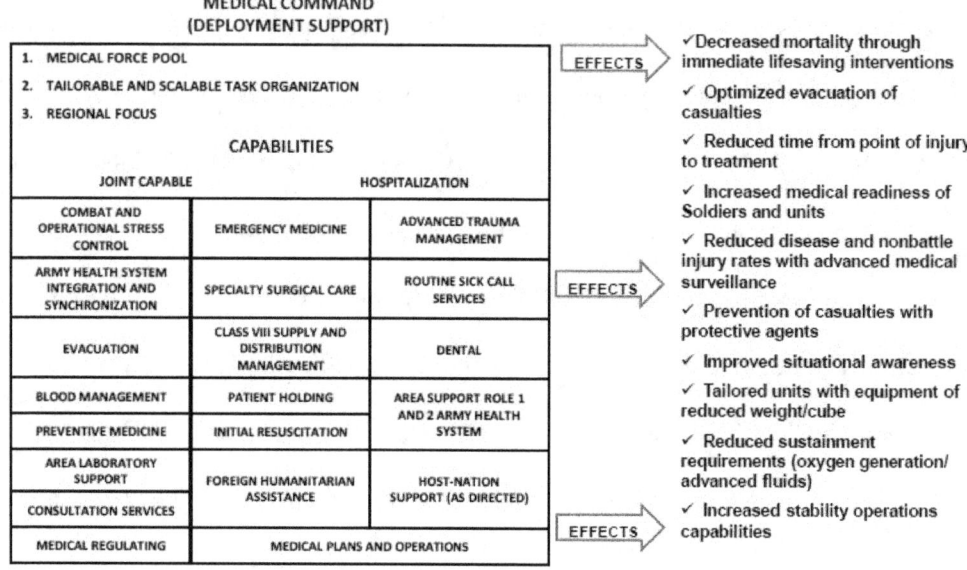

CAPABILITIES-BASED MODULES
(TAILORABLE AND SCALABLE)

Figure 2: U.S. Army medical capability based modules.[68]

The following year, the latest update to JP 4-02 *Medical Operations* explicity emphasises the

importance and considerations of using medical liaison officers to enable continuity between the

MHS relief effort and the afflicted nation's medical system.[69] It goes on to describe how a joint

force commander should assemble and apply humanitarian assistance survey teams.[70] The U.S.

Air Force concurently expanded its role in FDR during this time. With the publication a

document titled *Medical Operations*, the Air Force complimented JP 3-07.6 and embraced its

Relief, GTA 90-01-030 (Washington D.C.: Government Printing Office, 2011), ix.

[68]U.S. Department of the Army, *Army Health System,* ATTP 4-02 (Washington, D.C.: Government Printing Office, 2011), 1-4.

[69]U.S. Department of Defense, *Health Service Support,* JP 4-02 (Washington, D.C.: Government Printing Office, 2012), II-23.

[70]Ibid., II-32.

medical potential within FDR.[71] Drawing from the 2010 Hatian experience, the manual

sanctioned the rapid deployment of Air Force health systems as part of the greater MHS response

effort.[72] Development of the Army's FDR medical capacity continues in 2013 with three recent

additions. Army Technical Publication 4-02.5 incorperates the option of employing a "Hospital

Augmentation Team (Special)" into FDR operations. This independently deployable team of

community health providers is trained and equipped to support 10,000 civilians for up to 30-

days.[73] *Multi-Service Techniques for Civil Affairs Support to Foreign Humanitarian Assistance*

directs multi-service civil affairs teams towards assuming a leadership role in the planning,

coordination, and execution of humanitarian operations of every scale.[74] In August of 2013,

ATTP 4-02 was superceded by a new FM 4-02 (*Army Health System*). This document clarifies

how medical functions operate by abandoning the confusing "medical capabilities-based

modules" described earlier, with a much more lucid "system of systems" concept which is

brought together through medical mission command modules (see Figure 3). This manual also

emphasises an early-entry capability within various medical mission command structures.[75]

---

[71]The Air Force developed a predecessor to this document in 2002 however it was only released in draft, therefore it was not examined within this study.

[72]U.S. Department of the Air Force, *Medical Operations,* Air Force Doctrine Document 4-02 (Washington, D.C.: Government Printing Office, 2012), 29-32.

[73]U.S. Department of the Army, *Casualty Care,* ATP 4-02.5 (Washington, D.C.: Government Printing Office, 2013), 3-17.

[74]U.S. Department of the Army, *Multi-Service Techniques for Civil Affairs Support to Foreign Humanitarian Assistance,* ATP 3-57.20 (Washington, D.C.: Government Printing Office, 2013).

[75]U.S. Department of the Army, *Army Health System,* FM 4-02 (Washington, D.C.: Government Printing Office, 2013).

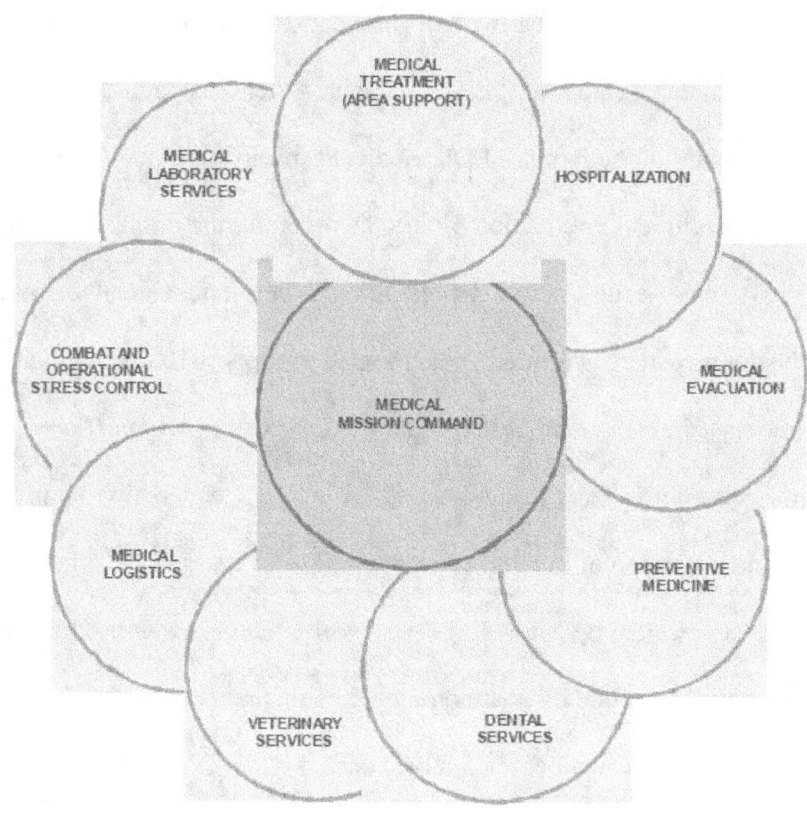

Figure 3: Medical "System of Systems" that are talorable and scalable under various mission command modules.[76]

If doctrine enhances the operational effectivness of the force "by providing fundamental principles that guide the employment of U.S. military forces toward a common objective," then doctrine and policy developed after the end of the Cold War portray a clear evolution and expansion of the MHS's capacity to respond to FDR.[77] This evolution did not occour without periods of trial and error. Four major FDR operations were instrumental in shaping the Unites

[76]U.S. Department of the Army, *Army Health System,* FM 4-02 (Washington, D.C.: Government Printing Office, 2013), 1-11.

[77]U.S. Department of Defense, *Doctrine for the Armed Forces of the United States,* JP 1 (Washington, D.C.: Government Printing Office, 2013), I-1.

States Government's perceptions towards the utilization of the MHS as a national humanitarian ambassodor. They are Operations Restore Hope, Unified Assistance, Lifeline, and Unified Response.

CASE STUDIES

Operation Restore Hope (Somalia, 1992)

We present Operation Restore Hope as one of the United States military's first post-Cold War FDR operations for two reasons. Somalia involved an incredible amount of human suffering and the ensuing humanitarian operation introduced the U.S. military to a relatively unfamiliar problem. Collective U.S. military actions within Somalia may be more accurately described as FHA, however the fate hundreds of thousands of civilians were in peril due to the international system's inability keep pace with the environment's demands. Global rivalries throughout the Cold War limited the political and military will to use military force to provide stability throughout the world.[78] As a result, there was little institutional knowledge within the DoD concerning the utility of health services towards the restoration of stability through the prevention of a humanitarian crisis.[79]

The cause of the Somali crisis can be directly attributed to a combination of manmade and natural events. Somalia was thrust into political existence in 1960 before its people had a clear sense of nationhood.[80] By the end of the Cold War, historically nomadic Muslim clans

---

[78]Kenneth Allard, *Somalia Operations: Lessons Learned* (Washington D.C.: National Defense University Press, 1995), 4.

[79]U.S. Department of the Army, *United States Forces After Action Review and Historical Overview: The United States Army in Somalia,* Center of Military History (Washington D.C.: 2003), 201.

[80]Walter S. Clarke, *Somalia: Background Information for Operation Restore Hope* (Carlisle Barracks, PA: U.S. Army War College, 1992), 9.

largely influenced the country's political dynamic.[81] Somali culture generally did not recognize political borders or physical barriers, which weakened the influence of the central government and resulted in strained relations with most of Somalia's neighbors.[82] The 1977 Ogaden War with Ethiopia irrevocably incapacitated the Somali Army to the point that it could no longer maintain domestic control. By early 1992, the central government collapsed after years of civil conflict with clans who sought to seize power.[83]

The country's infrastructure was decimated as a result of the civil strife. The modicum of agricultural capacity that survived the civil war was wiped out in 1992 when central and southern Somalia were hit with a severe drought. United Nations representatives estimated that one-quarter of Somalia's population (approximately 1.5 million people) was in danger of death by starvation. The international community responded, however relief efforts were complicated by bands of armed Somali men who would interdict food shipments. The actions of these men seemed to defy logic as they were frequently under the influence of a narcotic known as qat. This drug helped to suppress their own personal suffering but made them aggressive towards authority.[84]

The U.S. military's involvement in Somalia was incorporated into the United Nations Operation in Somalia (UNOSOM) effort on August 15, 1992 with Operation Provide Relief. This operation limited the number of American troops within Somalia by airlifting humanitarian relief supplies to neighboring Kenya and partitioning those supplies out to international relief agencies.

---

[81]Ibid., 6.

[82]Walter S. Clarke, *Somalia: Background Information for Operation Restore Hope* (Carlisle Barracks, PA: U.S. Army War College, 1992), 4.

[83]Ibid., 24-39.

[84]Helen Chapin Metz, ed., *Somalia: A Country Study,* 4th ed. (Washington D.C: Government Printing Office, 1993), xxx-xxxii.

This method quickly proved inadequate. Armed gangs pilfered relief convoys and seized supplies, which then became a source of power for warring clans. By December 3, the United Nations Security Council passed Resolution 794 authorizing the commitment of U.S. ground forces. [85] I Marine Expeditionary Force and the Army's 10th Mountain Division provided the bulk of the U.S. ground force component.[86] Thus began Operation Restore Hope.

Restore Hope was an international effort. Coalition forces were provided from 23 nations to work with 49 different relief organizations. As a result of the coalition military effort, 500,000 Somali patients were treated.[87] The U.S. Military's contribution to this figure was parsimonious when compared to other nations however. By September of 1993, a Moroccan military hospital treated its 100,000th Somali patient.[88] Contrarily, Somali admission to the U.S. Military hospital never rose above 28 during a single month.[89] The U.S. medical task force mission statement was to "Provide-coordinate medical support and service to the theater of operations" and offered no mention of the local human suffering.[90] Subsequent medical task-force mission statements were

---

[85]U.S. Department of the Army, "The United States Army in Somalia: 1992-1994." Department of Military History, http://www.history.army.mil/brochures/Somalia/Somalia.htm (downloaded 10 October, 2008), 8-10.

[86]Ibid., 9-10.

[87]U.S. Department of the Army, *United States Forces After Action Review and Historical Overview: The United States Army in Somalia,* Center of Military History (Washington D.C.: 2003), 23.

[88]Ibid., 102.

[89]There is no distinction of how many of these patients received injuries due to coalition force action.

[90]U.S. Department of the Army, *United States Forces After Action Review and Historical Overview: The United States Army in Somalia,* Center of Military History (Washington D.C.: 2003), 188.

modified to include care to "qualified" Somalis. Somali patients were only treated with the explicit approval of the hospital's Deputy Commander for Clinical Services.[91]

The U.S. military units outside of the medical task force provided health services to Somali citizens, but these services were limited in scope and scale when compared to the commitment of other nations. The 96th Civil Affairs Battalion conducted medical assessments early in the operation to identify medical requirements.[92] The 13th Marine Expeditionary Unit provided field medical and dental care to over 1,800 Somalis from October to December of 1993. While these activities formed a significant addition to the U.S. military medical effort, they did not significantly expand on the capabilities offered by NGOs-IGOs. After action comments suggest that U.S. military medical relief efforts were not well coordinated or well received by international relief agencies.[93] U.S. military medical forces concluded Operation Restore Hope in March of 1994 following the previous October's disastrous security operations.[94]

Operation Unified Assistance (Indonesia, 2004)

Operation Unified Assistance began as what may be described as a large scale, rapid onset natural disaster.[95] On December 26, 2004 at 6:58 a.m., the largest earthquake to hit the

---

[91]Ibid., 200.

[92]U.S. Department of the Army, *United States Forces After Action Review and Historical Overview: The United States Army in Somalia,* Center of Military History (Washington D.C.: 2003), 7.

[93]Lois M. Davis et al. *Army Medical Support for Peace Operations and Humanitarian Assistance* (Santa Monica, CA: RAND Corporation, 1996), 58.

[94]U.S. Department of the Army, *United States Forces After Action Review and Historical Overview: The United States Army in Somalia,* Center of Military History (Washington D.C.: 2003), 139.

[95]U.S. Department of Defense, *Department of Defense Support to Foreign Disaster Relief,* GTA 90-01-030 (Washington D.C.: Government Printing Office, 2011), 6-1.

world in 40 years struck 10 miles under the seabed off of the western tip of Indonesia's Sumatra Island.[96] The earthquake generated a tsunami that travelled between 600 to 800 kilometers per hour. Tidal waves as high as 20 meters struck the coastlines of 12 countries around the Indian Ocean. The largest of these waves hit the Indonesia's Aceh Province along western coast of Sumatra and swept nearly five kilometers inland, decimating the transportation infrastructure and isolating survivors from help. The local and provincial government response was paralyzed as offices and officials were swept away by the water. The scope of geographic damage and scale of the disaster was initially muted due to the lack of global media presence and the holiday weekend.[97] The Indonesian Government estimates that 125,866 souls were lost and an additional 419,682 were displaced.[98]

Indonesia's capacity to act was immediately overwhelmed. The disaster prompted an unprecedented military humanitarian response from around the world. The Government of Indonesia's request for assistance was open ended, with the stipulation that foreign military forces limit their plans to a 90-day operation.[99] Indonesian authorities had plenty of reason to be concerned over an enduring military presence in the Aceh Province. In 2004, the Indonesian government was still emerging from the shadow of a brutal anti-communist authoritarian regime.[100] Additionally, Aceh is situated on one of the busiest shipping lanes in the world, hosts

---

[96]U.S. Agency for International Development, *Tsunami Relief*, Report prepared by U.S. Agency for International Development (Washington D.C., April 2005).

[97]Bruce Ellman, "Waves of Hope: The U.S. Navy's Response to the Tsunami in Northern Indonesia" (monograph, Naval War College, 2007), 15-19.

[98]Sharon Wiharta et al., *The Effectiveness of Foreign Military Assets in Natural Disaster Response* (Solna, Sweden: The Stockholm International Peace Research Institute, 2008), 87-88.

[99]Ibid., 109-110.

[100]Angel Rabasa and Peter Chalk, *Indonesia's Transformation and the Stability of Southeast Asia*, (Santa Monica, CA: RAND, 2001) 27-37.

between 11 to 15 percent of Indonesia's natural resource exports, and is of strategic importance to Indonesia's allies and enemies.[101] Concerns over regional ethnic and religious extremist groups further complicated relief efforts. Due to its location as a geographic and cultural crossroad, Ache's predominantly Muslim population had a long history of rejecting outside influence and struggling for autonomy.[102] Local cries for independence were further fueled by feelings of exploitation by the central government. The Indonesian military had spent the preceding 30 years suppressing a provincial insurgency.[103]

The U.S. military's response was brisk. Within 24 hours, an operational planning team was stood up at United States Pacific Command (PACOM). By December 27, orders were issued dispatching the *USS Abraham Lincoln* Carrier Battle Group, the *USS Bon Homme Richard* Expeditionary Strike Group, and several Air Force and Navy aircraft to the area.[104] On December 28, the decision from PACOM was to stand up Combined Support Force (CSF) 536 in Utapao, Thailand. Two days later, a U.S. disaster relief assessment team was on the ground in Indonesia.[105] Throughout the initial stages of disaster response, perhaps the greatest medical

---

[101]One-quarter of the world's commerce flows through the Straights of Malacca. This makes it a strategic maritime lifeline to most of southeast Asia.

[102]In the mid-1970s, Acehnese organized under the Gerakan Aceh Merdeka (GAM) or Free Aceh Movement. The aim of this grassroots insurgency was to secure Aceh's independence.

[103]Angel Rabasa and Peter Chalk, *Indonesia's Transformation and the Stability of Southeast Asia* (Santa Monica, CA: RAND, 2001), 27-37.

[104]The presence of these naval task forces within a week introduced a substantial medical capability. According to *Jane's Fighting Ships*, the *USS Bon Homme Richard* is equipped with a 64-bed hospital and six operating rooms. The *USS Abraham Lincoln* is equipped with a small hospital, operating room, and ancillary medical services. Although there is little evidence that these facilities treated large numbers of victims, the medical personnel delivered treatment and supplies to the affected area.

[105]Paule Lefebvre, "Operation Unified Assistance," (Presentation, National Defense University 2005 Pacific Symposium, Waikiki, HI, June 10, 2005).

contribution was the arrival of rotary-wing airlift. While not designed for medical evacuation, helicopter crews evacuated several injured victims to triage points and Indonesian hospitals as well as delivering relief supplies.[106]

Not all of the DoD's medical lines of efforts were as decisive. A request for a rapidly deployable field hospital at Banda Aceh Airport was among the first requests by the Indonesian Government.[107] A draft deployment order was subsequently generated for the Pacific Air Force's Expeditionary Medical Support System (EMEDS) while the PACOM staff worked to define the requirement and worked to solve logistics issues.[108] Despite repeated requests from the Indonesian Government, these issues were never resolved. Confusion and inexperience among joint planners regarding the asset's capability, transportation, and support requirements delayed the deployment of the EMEDS until its presence was no longer relevant.[109]

One of the more iconic images from the DoD's medical response to Operation Unified Assistance was that of the *USNS Mercy* sailing off of the shores of Indonesia. This 1,000-bed vessel's presence introduced a significant self-contained hospitalization capability, while solving several political, social, and logistics issues through its design. Unfortunately, this very same design limited its relevance upon arrival. Home ported in San Diego, the *Mercy* was activated for service on January 1st and set sail on the 8th while supplies and personnel were still being

---

[106]Bruce Ellman, "Waves of Hope: The U.S. Navy's Response to the Tsunami in Northern Indonesia" (monograph, Naval War College, 2007), 61.

[107]The U.S. Embassy forwarded this request on December 27.

[108]An EMEDS is a scalable surgical facility designed and operated by the U.S. Air Force for rapid deployment. With all assigned modules deployed, it is roughly equivalent to a 25-bed Role III medical treatment facility.

[109]U.S. Department of the Air Force, *With Compassion and Hope: The Story of Operation Unified Assistance,* Headquarters, Pacific Air Forces Office of History (Hickam Air Force Base, HI, 2006), 18-22.

marshaled for service.[110] After stopping in Pearl Harbor and Singapore to take on additional personnel and supplies, the *Mercy* arrived off of the Indonesian coast on February 3.[111] Many of the medical personnel taken on during these port calls were civilian medical providers who were recruited through NGOs and IGOs.[112] This "novel idea" was an unprecedented step in military-NGO and IGO integration and came to be known as "The Mercy Model."[113] The action quickly generated a pool of tailored medical skillsets while preserving the DoD's limited number of healthcare providers for military specific operations.[114] The ship's presence also solved many of the force-protection, host-nation integration, and patient regulating issues that concerned medical planners. Personnel were ferried ashore daily to assist in assessment, triage, treatment, logistics, and medical regulating activities. These personnel were then recovered to the ship every evening.

The *Mercy's* contribution to the relief effort was by no means insignificant. By June 8, it had conducted 32,790 patient visits and conducted 466 surgeries.[115] Many of the medical services provided were associated with chronic conditions that were not associated with the tsunami.

---

[110]This was to be the *Mercy's* first operational deployment thirteen years. The ship departed San Diego with three hundred pallets of pallets of medical supplies predominantly configured for the treatment of combat trauma. Throughout its three month deployment, it took on an additional 1,800 pallets of medical supply configured for tsunami related humanitarian assistance.

[111]Paule Lefebvre, "Operation Unified Assistance," (Presentation, National Defense University 2005 Pacific Symposium, Waikiki, HI, June 10, 2005).

[112]Prior to integrating onto the *USNS Mercy*, civilian volunteers were given a crash shipboard orientation course on the Mercy's sister ship (*USNS Comfort*) at the Port of Baltimore, Maryland.

[113]Bruce Ellman, "Waves of Hope: The U.S. Navy's Response to the Tsunami in Northern Indonesia" (monograph, Naval War College, 2007), 83-86.

[114]Ibid.

[115]Paule Lefebvre, "Operation Unified Assistance," (Presentation, National Defense University 2005 Pacific Symposium, Waikiki, HI, June 10, 2005).

While the ship and crew performed admirably at filling a void that was created by the destruction of Indonesia's healthcare system, the ship's potential for influencing the acute emergency treatments associated with sudden onset disasters was diminished due to its month-long deployment cycle.[116]

The deployment of sea-based medical assets received mixed reviews. The deployment of the *USNS Mercy* satisfied acute domestic and international messages with minimal risk. The emergence of American global health diplomacy produced favorable local opinions of the United States throughout the affected area.[117] The action also sent a message to American competitors that it would not be easy to stand up to the United States' influence as a regional superpower.[118] Conversely, the enduring political benefit of this action has been questioned when compared to the costs. Further research on the long-term effects of health engagement to public opinion has been called for.[119]

Operation Lifeline (Pakistan, 2005)

An understanding of the 2005 Kashmir earthquake cannot be developed without first understanding the pre-existing complex conditions within the region. In broad terms, Kashmir is part of an 187,180 square kilometer former state known as Jammu and Kashmir.[120] Because

---

[116]Bruce Ellman, "Waves of Hope: The U.S. Navy's Response to the Tsunami in Northern Indonesia" (monograph, Naval War College, 2007), 81-82.

[117]Michael Smith, "A Better Disaster Response: Building a Solid Foundation" (Monograph, Naval War College, 2009), 4.

[118]Bruce Ellman, "Waves of Hope: The U.S. Navy's Response to the Tsunami in Northern Indonesia" (monograph, Naval War College, 2007), 103-105.

[119]Derek Licina, "Hospital Ships Adrift: A Systematic Literature Review Characterizing U.S. Navy Hospital Ship Humanitarian and Disaster Response," *Prehospital and Disaster Medicine 28*, no. 3 (July 2013): 1-9

[120]Teresita Schaffer, *Kashmir: The Economics of Peace Building* (Washington D.C.:

sections of Jammu and Kashmir are administratively controlled by Pakistan, India, and China, there is no consensus between these governments concerning the legitimacy of claims within Kashmir. Its political disposition has been a source of contention between the governments of Pakistan and India from the moment the two countries gained independence from Great Britain in 1947.[121] Two wars and several smaller but violent campaigns have been fought indecisively between the two countries over the territory.[122] In 2005, India and Pakistan were engaged in a cease-fire agreement, which eased tension throughout the relief effort.[123]

For the purpose of this case study, "Kashmir" will refer to the Pakistani administered province contemporarily known as Azad (Free) Jammu and Kashmir. Nestled in the Himalayan foothills, this area is the southern–most area of disputed territory administratively claimed and controlled by Pakistan. It is a rural and rugged sliver of land that extends 250 miles north to south, but only 10-40 miles exist between its undisputed border with Pakistan proper and a line of control to the east with Indian administered Kashmir.[124] The epicenter of the 2005 earthquake occurred in the vicinity of the provincial capital of Muzaffarabad.[125]

While the people within Kashmir are almost entirely Muslim, the language and culture of the area are distinct from greater Pakistan. Residents are more highly educated on average than

---

Center for Strategic and International Studies, 2005), 1.

[121]John Schmidt, *The Unraveling: Pakistan in the Age of Jihad* (New York: Picador, 2011), 9.

[122]Anatol Lieven, *Pakistan: A Hard Country* (New York: Public Affairs, 2011), 186.

[123]Sharon Wiharta et al., *The Effectiveness of Foreign Military Assets in Natural Disaster Response* (Solna, Sweden: The Stockholm International Peace Research Institute, 2008), 128.

[124]Michael LeFever, *Operation Lifeline After Action Report,* Combined Disaster Assistance Center Pakistan, (Washington, D.C.: Government Printing Office, 2006), 11.

[125]Teresita Schaffer, *Kashmir: The Economics of Peace Building* (Washington D.C.: Center for Strategic and International Studies, 2005), 3.

the rest of Pakistan, however they are usually poorer.[126] Agriculture and forestry are the primary

sources of income for residents. A network of paved roads cuts into the slopes of the surrounding

mountains, however the region has no direct access to rail or sea. Many of these roads were

severed in the 2005 quake due to landslides.[127]

Regional tensions with India and Afghanistan turned Kashmir into a haven for Islamic

extremists. Three primary jihadist groups had established spheres of influence. The focus of

these mujahedeen oscillated between undermining India's influence in the area, resisting the

establishment of a non-Taliban government in neighboring Afghanistan, and securing Kashmir's

independence from the central government of Pakistan.[128] The existence of these extremist

networks preoccupied a preponderance of U.S. military's attention towards Pakistan.[129] Just as in

Indonesia, the presence of these groups generated security concerns and questionable perceptions

of impartiality for western military responders.[130]

The 7.6 magnitude earthquake struck on October 8, 2005 at 8:50 a.m. (local).[131]

Hundreds of powerful aftershocks followed.[132] Pakistan's official statistics later put the total

---

[126]Observers believe that the egalitarian social structure of Kashmir encourages a higher aggregate level of education when compared against the feudal social tendencies of Pakistan.

[127]Teresita Schaffer, *Kashmir: The Economics of Peace Building* (Washington D.C.: Center for Strategic and International Studies, 2005), 29-36.

[128]John Schmidt, *The Unraveling: Pakistan in the Age of Jihad* (New York: Picador, 2011), 81-86.

[129]General John P. Abizaid, speaking for the 2005 posture of The United States Central Command, on March 1, 2005, to the Senate Armed Services Committee, 109th Cong., 1st sess.

[130]Sharon Wiharta et al., *The Effectiveness of Foreign Military Assets in Natural Disaster Response* (Solna, Sweden: The Stockholm International Peace Research Institute, 2008), 112.

[131]Due to the timing of the quake, many of the dead and injured were schoolchildren whose classrooms collapsed around them.

[132]Sharon Wiharta et al., *The Effectiveness of Foreign Military Assets in Natural Disaster*

dead at 73,338 with an additional 69,4112 seriously injured.[133] The regional medical structure was decimated. In total, 796 health facilities were destroyed and a further 119 were rendered unsafe.[134] With the onset of Himalayan winter approaching, it was apparent that a second wave of death would occur if immediate aid were not provided.[135] Offers from throughout the international community arrived before the Government of Pakistan made its first formal appeal on October 10.[136] Within eight hours of the earthquake, coalition military helicopters began arriving from Afghanistan.[137] It would be the first time that NATO forces participated in disaster relief operations outside of the Euro-Atlantic region.[138]

As Pakistan put out an international appeal for assistance, requests were tailored towards filling capability gaps that existed within the Pakistani Army's response.[139] Healthcare was never formally requested.[140] In spite of this, several countries provided military medical assets.[141] The

---

Response (Solna, Sweden: The Stockholm International Peace Research Institute, 2008), 107.

[133]Sharon Wiharta et al., *The Effectiveness of Foreign Military Assets in Natural Disaster Response* (Solna, Sweden: The Stockholm International Peace Research Institute, 2008), 107.

[134]Ibid., 115.

[135]Ibid., 107.

[136]Ibid.

[137]Ibid., 129.

[138]Ibid., 107.

[139]According to NATO's Euro-Atlantic Response Center Report dated October 8, the top two priorities were rescue/cargo helicopters and earth moving equipment for search and rescue operations.

[140]To be fair to relief organizations, it took the Pakistani Government weeks to identify the extent of damage and assess needs. While not specifically requested, aggressive employment of healthcare capabilities seems logical considering the level of destruction to Kashmir's medical infrastructure.

[141]Sharon Wiharta et al., *The Effectiveness of Foreign Military Assets in Natural Disaster*

U.S. military dispatched two field hospitals.[142] The 212th Mobile Army Surgical Hospital (MASH) arrived in Muzaffarabad on October 23 and established initial operating capacity within 12 hours.[143] The Combined Medical Relief Team from the Marine Corps III Marine Expeditionary Force (CMRT-3) arrived in Shinkiari on November 13 and was fully functional within 48 hours.[144] Word of the hospitals' presence spread quickly as reflected by the increase in treatments.[145] Combined, the two hospitals saw a total of 34,488 patients and performed 566 surgeries from October 23 to February 22.[146]

Both hospitals demonstrated agility with their medical logistics. Equipped to treat combat casualties, a great deal of effort was made towards adapting these units towards primary care services.[147] Initially, units often had to adapt medical equipment sets for pediatric populations until appropriate lines of medical supply could be established.[148] The CMRT-3 biomedical repair technicians even assisted a Cuban field hospital repair their malfunctioning X-ray equipment.[149] Upon the completion of their mission, the 212th MASH helped a newly

---

Response (Solna, Sweden: The Stockholm International Peace Research Institute, 2008), 131-135.

[142]Michael LeFever, *Operation Lifeline After Action Report,* Combined Disaster Assistance Center Pakistan, (Washington, D.C.: Government Printing Office, 2006), 45.

[143]Ibid., 47.

[144]Michael LeFever, *Operation Lifeline After Action Report,* Combined Disaster Assistance Center Pakistan, (Washington, D.C.: Government Printing Office, 2006), 51.

[145]Healthcare providers noted in the after action review that patients routinely walked many miles simply to be treated by a foreign doctor.

[146]Michael LeFever, *Operation Lifeline After Action Report,* Combined Disaster Assistance Center Pakistan, (Washington, D.C.: Government Printing Office, 2006), 124-128.

[147]Ibid., 46.

[148]Ibid., 48.

[149]Ibid., 53.

commissioned Pakistan Army medical battalion assume responsibility for recovery by

coordinating for the transfer of $4.7 million in military medical equipment.[150]

Aviation assets quickly established and maintained the ability to evacuate the injured.[151]

Within the first week, the relief task-force logged over 1,000 evacuations.[152] The intensity of

evacuation missions remained steady until the beginning of November.[153] By the end of March,

the NATO aviation task force reported a total of 3,754 evacuations.[154] While it is acknowledged

that these evacuations saved lives, Pakistani officials expressed concern that the movement of so

many victims to hospitals in Islamabad displaced civilians and unduly stressed the government.[155]

Despite the collection of an impressive measure of performance record, a review of the

measures of effectiveness returned mixed conclusions. Prior to the disaster, the standard of

healthcare within Kashmir was poor. The ratio of physicians to population was one-quarter of

Pakistan's average.[156] This encouraged unaffected locals to take advantage of the improved

standard in care. Confusion developed amongst medical providers around the fact that there was

---

[150]Michael LeFever, *Operation Lifeline After Action Report,* Combined Disaster Assistance Center Pakistan, (Washington, D.C.: Government Printing Office, 2006), 72.

[151]Reporting metrics within the task force's after action review and personal interviews indicate that the U.S. Army did not deploy aero-MEDEVAC platforms. Evacuations are reported as CASEVACs, however the report cites a partnership of "Parajumpers" with search and rescue aircraft from Luxembourg.

[152]Michael LeFever, *Operation Lifeline After Action Report,* Combined Disaster Assistance Center Pakistan, (Washington, D.C.: Government Printing Office, 2006), 83.

[153]Ibid., 118.

[154]Ibid., 112.

[155]William A. Mosier and Walter H. Orthner, "Military Medical Support for Humanitarian Assistance and Disaster Relief: Lessons Learned From the Pakistan Earthquake Relief Effort," *Joint Center for Operational Analysis* 9, no. 2 (June 2007): 7.

[156]Teresita Schaffer, *Kashmir: The Economics of Peace Building* (Washington D.C.: Center for Strategic and International Studies, 2005), 32.

no clear distinction between relief and rehabilitation work.[157] Within the first few weeks of the

relief effort, hospitals detected a significant shift from the treatment of emergent earthquake

related injuries towards the treatment of pre-existing chronic and elective treatments.[158]

Healthcare providers enthusiastically continued to provide free pharmaceuticals and a standard of

care that exceeded the local norm.[159] These actions further upset the local healthcare industry.[160]

Pakistani medical authorities lamented that in some instances, these well-intended efforts

produced more harm than good.[161]

As in Indonesia, the U.S. military's global health diplomacy initiatives helped have an

acute positive impact in the local population's perception of the United States. Polling indicates

that favorable opinions of the U.S. and unfavorable opinions of Osama Bin Laden doubled.[162]

Skeptics have argued that this is an example of the erosion of impartiality in humanitarian

principles.[163] It is worth mentioning that the Islamist terrorist organization Lashkar-e-Tabia

effectively used healthcare for the same means throughout Kashmir.[164]

---

[157] Sharon Wiharta et al., *The Effectiveness of Foreign Military Assets in Natural Disaster Response* (Solna, Sweden: The Stockholm International Peace Research Institute, 2008), 117.

[158] Michael LeFever, *Operation Lifeline After Action Report,* Combined Disaster Assistance Center Pakistan, (Washington, D.C.: Government Printing Office, 2006), 78.

[159] Sharon Wiharta et al., *The Effectiveness of Foreign Military Assets in Natural Disaster Response* (Solna, Sweden: The Stockholm International Peace Research Institute, 2008), 117.

[160] These activities resulted in the emergence of a pharmaceutical black market and forced many local doctors out of business. The Stockholm International Peace Institute reports that the affected population was unwilling to revert to the standard of care pre-existent to the earthquake.

[161] William A. Mosier and Walter H. Orthner. "Military Medical Support for Humanitarian Assistance and Disaster Relief: Lessons Learned From the Pakistan Earthquake Relief Effort," *Joint Center for Operational Analysis* 9, no. 2 (June 2007): 7.

[162] Michael LeFever, *Operation Lifeline After Action Report,* Combined Disaster Assistance Center Pakistan, (Washington, DC: Government Printing Office, 2006), 71.

[163] Wiley Thompson, "Perfect Strangers: An Examination of Contemporary Military

<u>Operation Unified Response (Haiti, 2010)</u>

In 2010, Haiti was already being described as a failed or fragile state.[165] Ever since the violent slave rebellion (of the late 18th and early 19th centuries) that secured its independence from France, Haiti's narrative had been associated with tumultuous political tension, social exploitation, and deplorable public health.[166] Common indicators ranked the Haitian standard of living among the worst in the world.[167] While signs of political and social improvement were beginning to emerge with the new millennium, the country's frailty was highlighted by a series of deadly hurricanes.[168] The summation of these forces decimated Haiti's domestic health capacity and abrogated responsibility for care to the international community.[169] Thousands of international relief organizations were already on the ground and overwhelmed in the days leading up to the earthquake.[170]

Involvement in Humanitarian Affairs," *Journal of Military Geography* Special Edition 1 (2010): 4.

[164]Anatol Lieven, *Pakistan: A Hard Country* (New York: Public Affairs, 2011), 195.

[165]Nicole Rencoret et al., *Haiti Earthquake Response: Context Analysis* (London: Active Learning Network for Accountability and Performance in Humanitarian Action Secretariat, July 2010), 9.

[166]William W. Mendel, "The Haiti Contingency," *Military Review* (January 1994): 49-50.

[167]In 2008-2009 statistics- Politics: 12th of 177 countries in Failed State Index; Economic: 149th of 182 countries in Human Development Index; 61 year life expectancy at birth.

[168]Nicole Rencoret et al., *Haiti Earthquake Response: Context Analysis* (London: Active Learning Network for Accountability and Performance in Humanitarian Action Secretariat, July 2010), 9-14.

[169]Ibid.,16-17.

[170]Laurent Dubois, *Haiti: The Aftershocks of History* (New York, NY: Metropolitan Books, 2012), 7.

The Haitian relationships with the U.S. military could erstwhile be described as tenuous.[171] Its strategic and political relevance to the United States correlates with the American ascension in global influence.[172] In the 20 years prior to the earthquake, the United States military had been a party to two major Haitian stability operations.[173] While U.S. military interventions within Haiti have been couched as humanitarian in nature, the ruling class did not always welcome these efforts.[174] Attempts to develop governance, security, infrastructure, and improve literacy were occasionally viewed as a threat to the prevailing social order.[175] Despite this, the commander of United States Southern Command (SOUTHCOM) touted the unified combatant command's success in disaster preparedness and medical engagement programs during his 2009 report to the Senate Armed Services Committee. Since 2007, SOUTHCOM had conducted three "Continuing Promise" medical engagement programs that treated over 385,000 patients throughout Central and South America.[176]

The presence and reliability of the United States military would prove decisive in the hours after the 7.0 magnitude earthquake struck on the January 12, 2010 just west of Port-au-Prince. An estimated 230,000 were killed and thousands more injured. Within hours, Haiti's

---

[171]Walter E. Kretchik, Robert F. Baumann, and John T. Fishel, *Invasion, Intervention, "Intervasion": A Concise History of the U.S. Army in Operation Uphold Democracy* (Fort Leavenworth, KS: Command and General Staff College Press, 1998), 7.

[172]Ibid.

[173]Nathaniel Crain, "Haiti: Two Decades of Intervention and Very Little to Show" (monograph, Command and General Staff College, 2012), 3.

[174]William W. Mendel, "The Haiti Contingency," *Military Review* (January 1994): 50.

[175]Walter E. Kretchik, Robert F. Baumann, and John T. Fishel, *Invasion, Intervention, "Intervasion": A Concise History of the U.S. Army in Operation Uphold Democracy* (Fort Leavenworth, KS: Command and General Staff College Press, 1998), 9

[176]Admiral Jim Stavridis, speaking for the 2009 posture of The United States Southern Command, on March 17, 2009, to the Senate Armed Services Committee, 111th Cong., 1st sess.

president dispatched several of his ministers by motorcycle to the home of the U.S. Ambassador. Through happenstance, the deputy commander of SOUTHCOM was already there and coordinating for the arrival of U.S. military assistance. What ensued was Operation Unified Response, the largest U.S. military foreign disaster response in history.[177]

Perhaps the most remarkable characteristics of the U.S. military's response were speed and resolve. The U.S. Air Force was decisive in land-force generation through the assumption of theater airspace management responsibilities and its ability to rapidly task and deploy strategic airlift.[178] Special operations surgical teams were among the first land-based surgical elements to arrive. They were followed shortly thereafter by a surgical team that had been forward deployed in Honduras.[179] These assets were soon augmented through enablers deployed by the Army's XVIII Airborne Corps and the 3rd Expeditionary Sustainment Command.[180] Later in the operation, these enablers would include medical logistics detachments that partnered with USAID in assisting the country at regaining control over its exhausted medical supply system.[181]

The U.S. Navy immediately redirected the *USS Carl Vinson*, *USS Bataan*, *USS Nassau*, and *USS Carter Hall* to move towards Haiti; each ship possessing respectable medical

---

[177]Ken Keen et al., "Foreign Disaster Response: Joint Task Force Haiti Observations," *Military Review* 90, no. 6 (2010): 85.

[178]NATO, *The Haiti Case Study*, (Lisbon: Joint Analysis and Lessons Learned Centre, 2012), A-1through A-2.

[179]Michele Hancock, "Medical Response to Haiti Earthquake: Operation Unified Response," (lecture, 2011 Military Health System Conference, National Harbor, MD, January 24, 2011).

[180]Ken Keen et al., "Foreign Disaster Response: Joint Task Force Haiti Observations," *Military Review* 90, no. 6 (2010): 86.

[181]NATO, *The Haiti Case Study*, (Lisbon: Joint Analysis and Lessons Learned Centre, 2012), A-4.

capability.[182] The carrier *USS Carl Vinson* arrived on January 15.[183] The *Vinson* brought with it a 47-man medical section, Carrier Air Wing 17, and a medical treatment facility. The command sent sailors ashore to assess and assist victims, conducted 435 evacuations, and saw 60 trauma patients aboard ship.[184] The *USS Bataan* arrived three days later with much more robust on-board medical treatment capability.[185] A medical team from the Bataan went ashore and embedded with an NGO clinic that had been in country since long before the earthquake. The sailors collaborated with the relief workers to establish the region's casualty collection point and triage patients for shore-to ship transfer. Within three weeks, the Bataan's corpsmen treated over 1,000 patients.[186] The *USS Carter Hall* sent corpsmen ashore to pair up with an international field hospital as well.[187]

The U.S. Navy staffed, equipped, and deployed the hospital ship *USNS Comfort* in an astonishing 76 ½ hours from verbal notice.[188] The "Mercy Model" was reinstituted and 244 non-

---

[182]Ken Keen et al., "Foreign Disaster Response: Joint Task Force Haiti Observations," *Military Review* 90, no. 6 (2010): 86.

[183]Michele Hancock, "Medical Response to Haiti Earthquake: Operation Unified Response," (lecture, 2011 Military Health System Conference, National Harbor, MD, January 24, 2011).

[184]Joel Carlson, "*USS Carl Vinson's* Medical Department Provides First Responder Care in Haiti," *Navy Medicine* 102, no 2. (210): 12.

[185]The *USS Bataan* maintains four operating rooms staffed by a fleet surgical team and additional corpsmen. One day after arriving in Haiti, the ship took on an additional 80 additional medical staff.

[186]Christina Shaw, "Bataan Medical Team Supports Haiti Relief," *Navy Medicine* 102, no 2. (2010): 22-24.

[187]Hendrick Dickson, "Navy Medicine Joins International Team at Haitian Field Hospital," *Navy Medicine* 102, no 2. (2010): 25-26.

[188]Adam Robinson, "Navy Medicine Supports Earthquake Relief," *Navy Medicine* 102, no 2. (2010): 4.

governmental healthcare providers were taken aboard.[189] The *Comfort* arrived on January 20, the same day as a magnitude 6.1 aftershock.[190] Upon arrival, she immediately became the country's most capable hospital.[191] Within the first 10-days off of the coast, her crew treated more than 540 critically injured patients. One physician remarked that the first week was completed in two 40-hour days separated by four-hours of sleep. At its peak, the *Comfort* was sustaining ten of her operating rooms at full capacity.[192] By the time the ship completed its mission on February 27, it had completed 843 surgeries.[193]

The U.S. Air Force deployed multiple surgical and medical evacuation related capabilities. On January 21, a mobile aeromedical staging facility and aeromedical evacuation team an arrived at Port-au-Prince Airport to prepare and coordinate victims for fixed-wing aeromedical evacuation. Five days later, a surgically capable EMEDS arrived and established itself in the vicinity of the seaport. This facility acted as the land-based "front and back door" to the *USNS Comfort* by triaging and repatriating the ships patients.[194]

---

[189]Cappy Surette, "Navy and Civilian Medical Teams Work Together to Provide Hope on Comfort," *Navy Medicine* 102, no 2. (2010): 20.

[190]Michele Hancock, "Medical Response to Haiti Earthquake: Operation Unified Response," (lecture, 2011 Military Health System Conference, National Harbor, MD, January 24, 2011).

[191]NATO, *The Haiti Case Study*, (Lisbon: Joint Analysis and Lessons Learned Centre, 2012), B-4.

[192]Tim Donohue, "Navy Medicine Hits the Blogosphere," *Navy Medicine* 102, no 2. (2010): 30.

[193]Shannon Warner, "USNS Comfort Crew Holds Ceremony for Haitians," *Navy Medicine* 102, no 2. (2010): 32-33.

[194]Michele Hancock, "Medical Response to Haiti Earthquake: Operation Unified Response," (lecture, 2011 Military Health System Conference, National Harbor, MD, January 24, 2011).

The scope and scale of the DoD's response may lead one to believe that it had wrestled responsibility away from USAID-OFDA. One policy maker remarked, "The U.S. military had 10,000 responders in the field, (USAID) had 34. The military was simply able to outrun everyone else."[195] In reality, DoD was arguably better embedded across the joint inter-agency, inter-governmental, and multi-national environment than any previous operation. A 2010 Government Accountability Office report acknowledged the stress that Operation Unified Response put the inter-agency under, but praised SOUTHCOM's 2009 theater campaign plan and organization for its ability to collaborate in the inter-agency environment.[196]

Military health services performed admirably throughout Operation Unified Response.[197] A few aspects of the DoD's response were identified for improvement however. The joint task force commander highlighted a substandard integration of medical planning in the operational approach.[198] The source of these challenges were attributed to organization and training. The SOUTHCOM staff was not staffed for sustained 24-hour operations. Once it was determined that the crisis would require a transition to sustained operations, faults were identified in SOUTHCOM's ability to requisition the required skill-sets.[199] It was further pointed out that the

---

[195]NATO, *The Haiti Case Study*, (Lisbon: Joint Analysis and Lessons Learned Centre, 2012), 18.

[196]U.S. Government Accountability Office, *Report to the Chairman, Subcommittee on National Security and Foreign Affairs, Committee on Oversight and Government Reform, House of Representatives,* GAO Document 10-801 (Washington, D.C., 2010), 14-25.

[197]The Joint Forces Commander's after action review reported that throughout the operation, over 19,000 earthquake victims were treated, 1,025 surgeries were performed, and 75 tons of medical supplies distributed.

[198]Joint Center for Operational Analysis, "Operation Unified Response: Haiti Earthquake Response" (after action review presentation, Norfolk, VA, May 15, 2010).

[199]U.S. Government Accountability Office, *Report to the Chairman, Subcommittee on National Security and Foreign Affairs, Committee on Oversight and Government Reform, House of Representatives,* GAO Document 10-801 (Washington, D.C., 2010), 14-25.

organic SOUTHCOM surgeon's staff was inadequately trained to integrate into the greater combatant command staff planning effort. [200] The joint force commander also expressed frustration at the inability to rapidly draw medical capabilities into the operational environment. While the XVIII Airborne Corps demonstrated a dynamic ability to deploy combat forces, similar preparations were not made for medical enablers. This resulted in delayed medical assessment and treatment.[201]

ANALYSIS

The heroic actions of military healthcare providers have touched countless lives during each of the disasters that have just been highlighted. The effectiveness of these efforts has varied however. In order to evaluate the success of these efforts, a model must be developed. By focusing on the emergency phase of disaster response, this monograph evaluates the efficacy of military medical care in relation to the preservation of life, limb, and eyesight injuries directly related to the event's effects. It will accomplish this by looking down two axis of logic. The first axis relates to medical activities that are in immediate demand following a disaster while the second relates to the relevance of those medical activities towards critically injured victims.

The first axis, will look at the military medical response to FDR through three of the U.S. Army's medical activities associated with the health service support warfighting function. They are evacuation, hospitalization, and medical logistics.[202] We have chosen these activities because

---

[200]Edwin Burkett and Jerry Tuero, "Developing Future Command Surgeons and Staff for Joint Operations Assignments," *Joint Center for Operational Analysis Journal 12,* no. 2 (2010): 51-54.

[201]Ken Keen et al., "Foreign Disaster Response: Joint Task Force Haiti Observations," *Military Review* 90, no. 6 (2010): 87-89.

[202]U.S. Department of the Army, *Army Health System,* ATTP 4-02 (Washington, D.C.: Government Printing Office, 2013) 7-1.

they are among the most urgent of requirements. This urgency is acknowledged within the United States National Disaster Medical Response System. It consists of three components that parallel the selected military medical activities. They are:

- "Medical Response to a disaster area in the form of personnel, teams and individuals, supplies, and equipment."
- "Patient Movement from a disaster site to unaffected areas of the nation."
- "Definitive medical care at participating hospitals in unaffected area."[203]

While domestic healthcare systems are agile enough to affect a positive outcome, conventional thought has conditioned us to believe that large-scale international emergency medical response would be ineffective because of complexity, time, and space.[204] This perceived gap has subdued the will of medical planners to project these capabilities into a foreign disaster environment. A response that can project urgent care capability before the perishability on its relevance is reached can greatly reduce human suffering. It is for this reason that this monograph looks at the aggregate of these three activities to identify measurable improvements in disaster response.

The second axis expresses the relevance of medical activities as tied to the military principles of health service support. In joint health service support doctrine, there are six principles of health support.[205] This monograph examines the efficacy of medical activities through the principles of proximity, flexibility, and continuity. These three principles are closely associated with quickly placing the right capability in the right place while complimenting the

---

[203]U.S. Department of Health and Human Services, *National Disaster Medical System Federal Coordination Center Guide,* (Washington, D.C., 2010), 7-8.

[204]Joint Center for Operational Analysis, "Humanitarian Assistance and Disaster Relief Lessons Information Paper" (Information paper, Norfolk, VA, 2010), 2.

[205]Joint Publication 4-02 states that the principles of health service support are conformity, proximity, flexibility, mobility, continuity, and control.

relief operations of the host nation and adjacent relief organizations.[206] These attributes are critical to a foreign disaster relief operation and have consequently been chosen as the measures of effectiveness.[207]

At the convergence of these two axes is a qualitative assessment of how well medical activities performed when compared to the health service support principles. A summary of medical activities within each operation is provided. This was made possible through the review of assorted critiques of each FDR action from various authors and organizations. As each medical activity was referenced a plus (+) was assigned for positive comments, minus (-) for negative comments, and plus/minus (+/-) for balanced groups of statements. Due to the irregularity of documentation, every medical activity could not consistently be assessed with the same level of fidelity. Every effort was made to represent each activity with comparable weight. The cumulative qualitative assessment of each principle is expressed using a "Red-Amber-Green" classification system. Red is used to express predominately negative comments. Amber is used for an aggregate of neutral or mixed comments. Green is used to express predominately positive comments.

Operation Restore Hope (Somalia, 1992)

The famine that triggered Operation Restore Hope was a slow onset, complex disaster. Although the disaster emerged slowly, there was no shortage of human suffering following abrupt international intervention. This case study illustrates the ambiguity that military medical personnel faced immediately following the Cold War. Military doctrine had just begun to

---

[206]U.S. Department of Defense, *Health Service Support,* JP 4-02 (Washington D.C.: Government Printing Office, 2012), I-1.

[207]Joint Center for Operational Analysis, "Humanitarian Assistance and Disaster Relief Lessons Information Paper" (Information paper, Norfolk, VA, 2010), 1-2.

acknowledge the utility of military force in operations other than war. The U.S. healthcare staff in Mogadishu was augmented in anticipation for possible humanitarian operations, however medical plans and assets were inflexibly oriented on Cold War era combat.[208] The apparent lack of will to care for the population was exacerbated by a lack of doctrine to support medical humanitarian relief actions.[209] While adjacent coalition hospitals treated hundreds of thousands of Somali patients, U.S. military providers struggled to develop an ad hoc humanitarian role that lacked potency.[210] The activities of these hospitals imply that acceptable conditions existed to reach out to the population. Attempts were made towards reaching out to relief organizations, however the cool reception that they received implies that these efforts were haphazardly coordinated.[211] Aero-MEDEVAC operations were limited to support coalition forces and UNOSOM civilians only.[212] This lack of engagement neutralized any benefit that the U.S. hospital gained through its forward location in the Mogadishu embassy compound.[213]

---

[208]Lois M. Davis et al. *Army Medical Support for Peace Operations and Humanitarian Assistance* (Santa Monica, CA: RAND Corporation, 1996), 77-80.

[209]U.S. Department of the Army, "United States Forces After Action Review and Historical Overview: The United States Army in Somalia," Center of Military History (Washington D.C.: 2003), 201.

[210]Lois M. Davis et al. *Army Medical Support for Peace Operations and Humanitarian Assistance* (Santa Monica, CA: RAND Corporation, 1996), 55-60.

[211]Ibid., 58.

[212]U.S. Department of the Army, "United States Forces After Action Review and Historical Overview: The United States Army in Somalia," Center of Military History (Washington D.C.: 2003), 170.

[213]Lois M. Davis et al. *Army Medical Support for Peace Operations and Humanitarian Assistance* (Santa Monica, CA: RAND Corporation, 1996), 60.

Table 1: Assessment of Operation Restore Hope

Proximity (Red)	Flexibility (Red)	Continuity (Red)
(-) Lack of care negated proximity to population	(-) Lack of understanding on equipment required for humanitarian operations (-) Lack of operational medical rules of engagement	(-) Haphazard integration with NGO-IGO presence (-) Lack of central government to coordinate with

Operation Unified Assistance (Indonesia, 2004)

A lot changed in the decade between Operation Restore Hope and Operation Unified Assistance. This evolution was reflected in the development of doctrine that captured and codified lessons learned from Operation Restore Hope into multi-service operational doctrine.[214] While this outgrowth of knowledge helped frame the U.S. military's role in FDR, it lacked the specificity to guide medical planners in developing an operational approach to healthcare. This equated to a new will to engage foreign disaster with military medicine, however actions proved mediocre when viewed through the principles of health service support.

The coincidental transition of the *USS Abraham Lincoln* Carrier Battle Group and *USS Bon Homme Richard* Expeditionary Strike Group transformed chance into serendipitous opportunity. Aggressive action on the part of the crews carried the day thereafter. This armada enabled hundreds of casualty evacuation flights within the first week of the disaster.[215] While the *Abraham Lincoln* possessed the capacity to preform emergency surgery, medical sections went

---

[214]The rapid establishment of crisis action planning groups, commitment of disaster assistance teams, and establishment of a combined support force demonstrated the military's growing operational confidence in FDR contingency operations.

[215]U.S. Agency for International Development, "Tsunami Relief," Report prepared by U.S. Agency for International Development (Washington D.C., April 2005), 13.

ashore to partner in a triage role with local relief organizations.[216] Robust hospitalization

capability arrived with the *USNS Mercy*, although its late arrival limited relevance towards

disaster related care. What the *USNS Mercy* lost in proximity, it gained in continuity. The 90-

day limit set by the Indonesian government at the onset of the disaster framed the environment for

planners to maintain the appropriate level of care and medical regulation at the right time

throughout the duration if the *Mercy's* time on station.[217] Additionally, the *Mercy's* crew broke

new ground in its partnership with non-governmental relief organizations.

Consternation on behalf of operational planners surrounding the employment of the

EMEDS equated to lost opportunity. Forward logistics units were responsive in surging medical

supplies to the affected area after the first week, although they struggled to deliver the type and

amount of supplies necessary for the moment.[218] Wholesale deliveries did not arrive until weeks

later on the *USNS Mercy* after two port calls to take on additional medical relief supplies and

personnel.

Table 2: Assessment of Operation Unified Assistance

Proximity (Amber)	Flexibility (Green)	Continuity (Green)
(+) Evacuation capability within 1st week (+/-) USNS Mercy hospitalization and resupply after 3 weeks (-) No EMEDS	(+/-) Medical resupply aggressive, but difficulty generating humanitarian lines of supply (+) Appropriate standard of care for duration of operation	(+) Triage and medical regulating integrated with host nation (+) NGOs IGOs integrated into USNS Mercy

---

[216]Joaquin Juatai, "*USS Abraham Lincoln* Medical Teams Provide Support in Banda Aceh" *Navy Medicine* 96, no.2 (2005): 10-13.

[217]John Bessler, "Defining Criteria for Handover to Civilian Officials in Relief Operations" (master's thesis, U.S. Army War College, 2008), 23-25.

[218]Amanda Woodhead, "USNH Okinawa Sends Medical Relief and Supplies to Southeast Asia" *Navy Medicine* 96, no.2 (2005): 6-7.

<u>Operation Lifeline (Pakistan, 2005)</u>

Almost a year later, medical planners had the benefit of learning from Operation Unified

Assistance when called upon to deploy assets to Operation Lifeline. It is not surprising that the

U.S. Navy pioneered detailed FDR health service support planning doctrine within that year and

large-scale disaster relief training exercises were being conducted.[219] The principle of proximity

captures the single greatest advantage to Operation Lifeline. The NATO presence in adjacent

Afghanistan sped the arrival of evacuation and logistics assets within a day of onset.

Hospitalization assets aggressively deployed, however were slower to respond due to the

restricted terrain and distances traveled. The first hospital assets arrived just over two weeks

from the disaster's onset.[220] As admission records indicate, this was scarcely inside the limit of

time required to provide relevance to earthquake related injuries.[221] While the hospitals were

successful at improvising supplies and equipment for community healthcare, delays were

experienced producing pediatric-specific materiel.

Continuity challenges were experienced across the board and the medical line of effort

overreached. While the medical measures of performance appear impressive, the measures of

effectiveness indicate that medical relief could have been better integrated into the host-nation's

vision for support. The introduction of U.S. standards of care did not integrate well with the local

economy. Free pharmaceuticals created a black market and aggressive evacuation created

---

[219]U.S. Department of the Navy, *Humanitarian Assistance/Disaster Relief Operations Planning,* NWDC TACMEMO 3-07.6-05 (Washington D.C.: Government Printing Office, 2005), chap 8.

[220]Michael LeFever, *Operation Lifeline After Action Report,* Combined Disaster Assistance Center Pakistan, (Washington, D.C.: Government Printing Office, 2006), 47.

[221]Ibid.,78.

displaced civilians.[222] Continuity rebounded at the conclusion of the mission with the training

and equipping of host-nation medical capability through the transfer of a U.S. hospital's

equipment to the Pakistani military.[223] This could not have been possible if it were not for the

pre-established working relationship between U.S. and Pakistani forces.[224]

Table 3: Assessment of Operation Lifeline

Proximity (Green)	Flexibility (Amber)	Continuity (Red)
(+) Evacuation and logistics capability within 1st day (+/-) Hospitalization on ground within three weeks	(+/-) Medical resupply aggressive, but difficulty generating humanitarian lines of supply (+) Evacuation prevented second wave of environmental casualties (-) Lack of operational medical rules of engagement	(-) Hospitalization damaged local health industry (-) Free medical supplies damaged local health industry and created black market (-) Evacuation created displaced persons (+) Well established partnership with Pakistani Army

Operation Unified Response (Haiti, 2010)

By 2010, the U.S. military's understanding of its potential towards FDR was well

reflected within joint military doctrine, policy, and strategy.[225] Operation Unified Response

demonstrated a growth in the conceptual possibilities of health services in FDR. Under the three

principles, health service support activities preformed admirably in two of three areas. The

---

[222]William A. Mosier and Walter H. Orthner, "Military Medical Support for Humanitarian Assistance and Disaster Relief: Lessons Learned From the Pakistan Earthquake Relief Effort," *Joint Center for Operational Analysis* 9, no. 2 (June 2007): 8-9.

[223]Michael LeFever, *Operation Lifeline After Action Report,* Combined Disaster Assistance Center Pakistan, (Washington, D.C.: Government Printing Office, 2006), 72.

[224]Sharon Wiharta et al., The Effectiveness of Foreign Military Assets in Natural Disaster Response (Solna, Sweden: The Stockholm International Peace Research Institute, 2008), 41.

[225]*JP 3-29: Foreign Humanitarian Assistance*, DODI 3000.05: Stability Operations, and the 2009 U.S. Southern Command Posture Statement.

principle of proximity was certainly enhanced by Haiti's vicinity to the United States. Nevertheless, response actions were immediate and resolute by any standard. Within hours, special operations medical teams were encountering patients on the ground. Within days, evacuation assets and medical relief supplies from the U.S. Navy arrived. Within a week, the U.S. military was operating the most capable hospital with in the affected area. It would more accurate to say that continuity was maintained verses established. Haitian officials had grown comfortable with U.S. military medical engagements and disaster preparedness exercises over previous years. This allowed rapid integration of healthcare teams.[226] Air Force patient administrators were put in place to ensure that thousands of victims were regulated between the U.S. military and host nation healthcare system as required. NGOs-IGOs converged on and integrated into the U.S. military's medical footprint in a remarkable example of civil-military cooperation. Perhaps most importantly, once the environment was stabilized the Department of Defense executed a controlled retrograde of medical capability that did not outlast its welcome.

The response to Haiti was unquestionably dynamic. As new requirements emerged, the medical capability was shifted. As capacity at Port-au-Prince airfield increased, the U.S. Air Force established a staging facility that regulated fixed wing medical evacuations to other countries. By the end of the disaster's first month, an Army multi-functional medical battalion was on the ground to supplement ground evacuation operations and assume management of the national medical supply warehouse. Flexibility was not seamless however. Shortfalls on the combatant commands medical staff prevented the operation from reaching its full potential early in the operation. The U.S. Southern Command's surgeon's cell found itself undermanned and

---

[226]NATO, *The Haiti Case Study*, (Lisbon: Joint Analysis and Lessons Learned Centre, 2012), 17.

undertrained to adequately integrate into the staff planning effort.[227] The joint task force commander later noted that while the immediate medical relief effort was "modest" and saved lives, it could have been much more aggressive early in the operation. The lack of a pre-designated expeditionary joint medical response teams hindered the DoD's ability to quickly develop a medical common operating picture.[228]

Table 4: Assessment of Operation Unified Response

Proximity (Green)	Flexibility (Amber)	Continuity (Green)
(+) Evacuation and logistics capability within two days	(+) Smooth transition from emergent to rehabilitative care	(+) Well established engagement history with GoH, NGOs, IGOs
(+/-) Hospitalization on ground within one week	(-) COCOM Surgeon staff under resourced to integrate response actions	(+) Well coordinated patient regulation

Summary of Findings

The overall analysis reveals an aggregate improvement in the efficacy of MHS in FDR environments. The most consistent improvement has been in the DoD's ability to place MHS assets in the proximity of the victims. The most distinguishing characteristic that has enabled this appears to be the decisiveness on the part of the combatant commander. His immediate choice to commit early-entry MHS to the response enabled assets to arrive when and where they were most relevant. This evolution of decisiveness correlates to the level of specificity and permissiveness of FDR policy and doctrine available at the time of the decision.

---

[227]Edwin Burkett and Jerry Tuero, "Developing Future Command Surgeons and Staff for Joint Operations Assignments," *Joint Center for Operational Analysis Journal 12,* no. 2 (2010): 51-54.

[228]Joint Center for Operational Analysis, "Operation Unified Response: Haiti Earthquake Response" (after action review presentation, Norfolk, VA, May 15, 2010), 196.

The ability to exercise flexibility and continuity has ebbed and flowed over the last two decades, but has demonstrated overall improvement as well. While there does not appear to be a single explanation for this fluctuation, a couple of trends exist that deserve exploration. Of the four disasters examined, three were within littoral zones.[229] Of these three, only Indonesia and Haiti benefitted from a sea-based medical response. While there were challenges involved with land-sea domain interface, the physical separation from the affected population and ability to maneuver hospitalization and air-launch platforms seems to have facilitated better flexibility and continuity. Physical separation provided security and prevented unintended impacts on the local healthcare system and culture. The ability to maneuver ensured that these MHS assets were able to transition healthcare resources to conform to changing requirements with ease.

In the cases of Pakistan and Haiti, the assessment of flexibility regressed from its all-time high during Operation Unified Assistance. In both of these cases, the flexibility of the medical response appears to have been limited by the dexterity of operational staff. In the case of Pakistan, medical rules of engagement were not developed at the operational level to support the desired state. Tactical practitioners were left to develop these rules for themselves without the resources to accurately evaluate the effect that their continued presence was having on the operational environment. In Haiti, the under-resourcing of the combatant command surgeon staff was cited as a limitation in the development of medical options for the joint task-force commander. This was later resolved through augmentation of the joint-manning document, however the delay appears to have affected the emergency phase of response.[230]

---

[229]For the purpose of this monograph, littoral zones are seacoasts and land within range of sea-based helicopters. Although Pakistan has littoral areas, the area surrounding Kashmir is outside of this zone.

[230]Joint Center for Operational Analysis, "Operation Unified Response: Haiti Earthquake Response" (after action review presentation, Norfolk, VA, May 15, 2010), 193-196.

Table 5: Overall assessment of the evolution of MHS in FDR

	Proximity	Flexibility	Continuity
Operation Restore Hope (Somalia, 1992)	Red	Red	Red
Operation Unified Assistance (Indonesia, 2004)	Amber	Green	Green
Operation Lifeline (Pakistan, 2005)	Green	Amber	Red
Operation Unified Response (Haiti, 2010)	Green	Amber	Green

It cannot be overstated that every disaster is unique. While it is impossible to prepare for every contingency, evidence indicates that there has been a fundamental change to the DoD's ability and approach towards deploying relevant and reliable health services to an affected area. Although the evidence indicates that this change occurred in consonance with the end of the Cold War, it is not the sole determinant. The efficacy of expeditionary health services is undeniably affected by larger systems. For example, the proliferation of cellular phones and social media has increased the capacity to rapidly assess requirements.[231] Replacement of the C-141 Starlifter with the C-17 Globemaster as the Air Force's primary inter-theater airframe improved the worldwide deployability of personnel and supplies.[232] The civilianization of global positioning systems has accelerated the ability to anticipate and pinpoint mass casualty events.[233] Individually, these breakthroughs have generated acute lifestyle modifications. Collectively, these advancements

---

[231]Mohammad-Ali Abbasi et al., "Lessons Learned in Using Social Media for Disaster Relief" (paper presented at the International Conference on Social Computing, Behavioral-Cultural Modeling, and Prediction, College Park, MD, April 3-5, 2012).

[232]U.S. Department of the Air Force, *Air Mobility Planning Factors,* Air Force Pamphlet 10-1403 (Washington D.C.: Government Printing Office, 2003), 10.

[233]Reinhard Kaiser et al., "The Application of Geographic Information Systems and Global Positioning Systems in Humanitarian Emergencies: Lessons Learned, Programme Implications, and Future Research," *Disasters*, 27, no. 2 (2003): 127-140.

have revolutionized the application of health services in FDR. This has not only improved the efficacy of military health systems; it has instituted a paradigm shift of the international community's impression of global health diplomacy.[234]

OBSERVATIONS

Regardless of whether strategists view the world through the realist or idealist lens, it can be agreed that development of the military's disaster relief capability is good for the United States.[235] To this point, this monograph has sought to portray whether MHS have evolved within a new epoch of global health engagement. By establishing that the efficacy of these systems has increased we can anticipate the future operational environment, the application of U.S. military forces within that environment, and the resources required for that application. This drives strategy. As General Martin Dempsey recently stated, "Strategy is about prediction, context, and choice."[236] Based on the trends and evidence that this monograph has provided, it may be worthwhile to speculate how the joint-force could better train, organize, and equip to meet this strategy.

Training

As demonstrated within the literature review, healthcare providers and planners have increasingly mature doctrine to guide them through FDR planning. In spite of this, a few recurring training shortfalls seem to emerge following major disasters. The first is on the part of

---

[234]Edwin Burkett, "Foreign Sector Capacity Building and the U.S. Military," *Military Medicine*, 177, no. 3 (2012): 298.

[235]James Miller, "Public Diplomacy and Foreign Disaster Relief: Machiavellian or Altruistic Approach?" (Research paper, U.S. Army War College, 2011), 7-8.

[236]Martin Dempsey, address at Duke University, January 2012, http://www.jcs.mil/speech.aspx?id=1673 (accessed July 29, 2013).

combatant command surgeon staffs. Some have argued that military medical culture overemphasizes clinical competence against operational experience.[237] This is a natural phenomenon, as specialization is desired within the tactical organizations that the DoD assigns junior medical officers to. These organizations are specialized and mechanistic within themselves. While efficient at performing straightforward tasks, specialization inhibits the flexibility required within strategic organizations that are assigned broader tasks.[238] As medical officers advance, this culture produces combatant command surgeon staffs that are disengaged from the joint operation planning and execution system.[239] Military medical culture consists of a series of silos layered within one another (see Figure 4).[240] Each layer inhibits what is sometimes described as "knowing in action." That is a level of familiarity that enables practitioners to demonstrate the reflexive competence required under urgent conditions.[241]

---

[237]Edwin Burkett and Jerry Tuero, "Developing Future Command Surgeons and Staff for Joint Operations Assignments," *Joint Center for Operational Analysis Journal 12,* no. 2 (2010): 51.

[238] Gareth Morgan, *Images of Organization* (Thousand Oaks, CA: Sage Publications, 2006), 27-29

[239]Joint Center for Operational Analysis, "Operation Unified Response: Haiti Earthquake Response" (after action review presentation, Norfolk, VA, May 15, 2010), 195.

[240] Mary Jo Hatch, *Organization Theory: Modern, Symbolic, and Postmodern Perspectives,* 2nd ed. (New York: Oxford University Press, 2006), 176.

[241]Donald Schon, *Educating the Reflective Practitioner* (San Francisco: Jossey-Bass, 1987), 25.

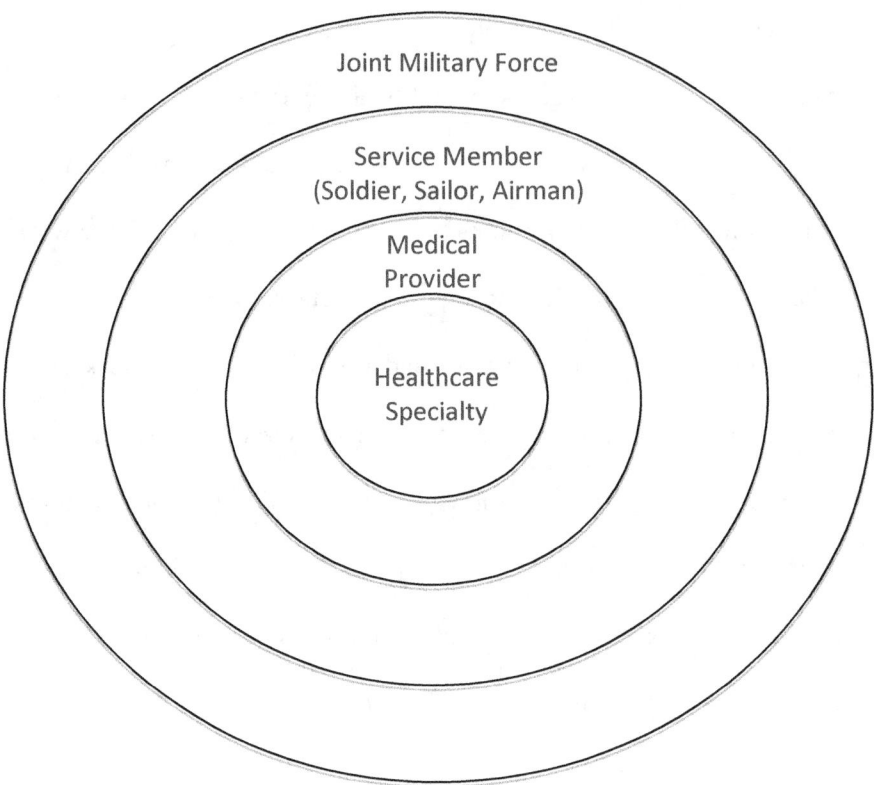

Figure 4: Military Medical Provider Cultural Silos.

Organizational theorists argue that performance in complex organizations is improved when specialization is balanced with integration.[242] One suggestion for achieving integration would involve a change to the values of military medical culture through the renovation of personnel management systems.[243] An amendment to the Goldwater-Nichols Act removing the joint-duty assignment waiver for medical personnel may encourage military healthcare providers to seek joint and operational assignment experience.[244] This would facilitate dynamic integration of joint military heath systems in the development operational approaches to FDR.

---

[242]Mary Jo Hatch, *Organization Theory: Modern, Symbolic, and Postmodern Perspectives.* 2nd ed. (New York: Oxford University Press, 2006), 112-113.

[243]Ibid., 104 and 186.

[244]*Goldwater-Nichols Department of Defense Reorganization Act of 1986*, Public Law

Additional training shortfalls have been attributed to a low emphasis on medically oriented exercises.[245] As combatant commanders increasingly incorporate FDR into their posture statements, training must follow.[246] This may be accomplished through a couple of training venues. First, medical actions should become a centerpiece of more staff training injects. This would keep both commanders and surgeon staffs attune to their mutually supporting relationships.[247] Second, scheduling of large-scale humanitarian and civic assistance operations should be expanded. The medical knowledge and interagency relationships developed through programs such as U.S. Southern Command's "Continuing Promise" generates international disaster preparedness and U.S. military medical providers who are skilled in international community health issues.[248]

Organization

As mentioned, the specialization of MHS has presented challenges to the efficiency of the DoD since the end of World War II. One repeatedly proposed solution to this problem lies within the creation of a joint military medical command. This could be accomplished through the

---

433, 99th Cong., 2nd sess. (October 1, 1986), § 404.

[245]Edwin Burkett and Jerry Tuero, "Developing Future Command Surgeons and Staff for Joint Operations Assignments," *Joint Center for Operational Analysis Journal 12,* no. 2 (2010): 52-53.

[246]In 2013, every geographic combatant command incorporated some form of FDR into their posture statements.

[247]Edwin Burkett and Jerry Tuero, "Developing Future Command Surgeons and Staff for Joint Operations Assignments," *Joint Center for Operational Analysis Journal 12,* no. 2 (2010): 52-53.

[248]U.S. Government Accountability Office, *Report to the Chairman, Subcommittee on National Security and Foreign Affairs, Committee on Oversight and Government Reform, House of Representatives,* GAO Document 10-801 (Washington, D.C., 2010), 36-40.

development of some type of joint service health service organization.[249] One of the goals of this organization would be to enhance the medical interoperability between the service components. The DoD's Task Force on Military Health System Governance conducted a study that examined four options towards implementing this change. While no single course of action stood out as the best for interoperability, the study concluded that the current arrangement impedes medical interoperability between services.[250] The establishment of a military joint health service organization could be supported by the aforementioned amendment to the Goldwater-Nichols Act.

Surgical capabilities may be pushed down to medical echelons below hospitals to rapidly introduce lifesaving surgical capability to the FDR environment. Within the U.S. and NATO MHS, the echelon of medical care between hospitals and front line maneuver units is known as Role II. This echelon is generally characterized by limited x-ray, operational dental support, combat-operational stress control, clinical laboratory, and limited patient holding capabilities. Many of these tasks are hospital-like, but performed at lower capacity. The Role II cluster of capabilities is organic to most of the U.S. Army's brigade combat teams. Within NATO doctrine, Role II automatically implies that forward surgical care capability will be present. The U.S. military doctrine does not reflect the same certainty.[251] This means that rapidly deployable organizations such the Army's Global Response Force do not consistently maintain surgical assets within their organic Role II medical treatment facilities. As demonstrated in Haiti, the

[249]Susan Hosek and Gary Cecchine, *Reorganizing the Military Health System: Should there be a Joint Command* (Santa Monica, CA: Rand National Security Research Division, MR-1350-OSD, 2001), xi-xiv.

[250]U.S. Department of Defense, *Task Force on Military Health System Governance Final Report,* (Washington, D.C., 2011), 32-33.

[251]U.S. Department of the Army, *Army Health System,* ATTP 4-02 (Washington, D.C.: Government Printing Office, 2013), 1-15.

Global Response Force is ideally suited for rapid reaction employment towards foreign disasters.[252] Organizing an organic surgical capability into rapid response Role II medical treatment facilities would not only improve interoperability with NATO partners, but would undoubtedly increase the relevance of the brigade combat team in an FDR environment.

All of the case studies looked at aerial evacuation of victims to hospitalization. Although every case study except Somalia demonstrated a level of success in providing this capability, none of them provided the type of en-route medical care associated with Army MEDEVAC. While en-route care may have been provided, the research indicates that this was predominantly ad hoc care provided on non-standard platforms. This may have been due, in part, to the reliance on sea basing within the majority of the case studies. The U.S. Naval forces do not maintain designated Aero-MEDEVAC platforms. As the lead agency for shore-to-ship and ship-to-shore transfers, the DoD may improve FDR survivability by either organizing forward deployed Army MEDEVAC detachments that remain afloat with the Navy and Marine Corps or the allowing for the proliferation of standard MEDEVAC platforms to other services.[253] Integrating Army MEDEVAC aboard Navy ships could be further enhanced through the joint medical integration initiatives mentioned earlier in this chapter.

Equipping

As we look towards the future, technology offers limitless opportunities to further improve MHS disaster response. While the purpose of this monograph is not to make a case for a specific platform, historical trends reveal the consistent success of some capabilities relating

---

[252]Charles Flynn and Joshua Richardson, "Joint Operational Access and the Global Response Force: Redefining Readiness," *Military Review* XCIII, no. 4 (2013), 42.

[253]Eric Shirly, "Joint Aeromedical Evacuation: Why Isn't it Adequate for the Combat Zone?" (master's thesis, Naval War College, 2004), 5.

directly to evacuation, hospitalization, and medical logistics. Disasters occur in many different forms, however all of them must occur on land where people are concentrated. All of the case studies following Operation Restore Hope have demonstrated the requirement to obtain lines of operation, operational reach, basing, and tempo over the collective domains of land, sea, and air. This requirement is one of the DoD's greatest challenges. When done well, the ability to meet this requirement has also generated some of the greatest opportunities for success.[254]

Hospitalization continues to be a challenge due to size and external sustainment requirements.[255] In Indonesia and Haiti, the U.S. Navy's two 1,000-bed Mercy Class hospital ships mitigated these adversities by providing sustainable Role III facilities outside of the disaster area. These ships do present their own limitations however. Mercy Class ships take up to five-days to get underway from port, may only accommodate one helicopter at a time, travel at a modest 17.5 knots, and have such a deep draft that they normally remain at least one-mile off coast. Both vessels are approaching their 40th year of service and may need to be retired in the foreseeable future.[256] Prior to the Indonesian tsunami, discussion was afoot to retire the hospital ship program in favor of shore based surgical teams.[257] Since that time, FDR and humanitarian

_____

[254]It is assumed that the proposed capabilities would improve combat readiness as well as FDR efficacy.

[255]According to ATP 4-02.5 (2013), the Army's planning factors for a 248-bed combat support hospital include 9.3 acres of cleared space and 13,115.35 gallons of potable water per day. It cannot transport, sustain, or secure itself without external support.

[256]Military Factory, "USNS Comfort (T-AH-20) Medical Support Vessel," http://www.militaryfactory.com/ships/detail.asp?ship_id=USNS-Comfort-TAH20 (accessed October 5, 2013).

[257]Christopher Munsey, "Navy medicine moves closer to combat zone- Hospital ships likely to retire, surgical teams head ashore in new plan to treat wounded," *Navy Times*, August 9, 2004.

assistance missions have brought about a revival in the utilization of these hospitals.[258] Indeed, other nations have taken notice. Some have speculated that China recently commissioned its 11th hospital ship (*Peace Ark*) in response to the DoD's ability to project "smart power."[259] The efficacy of the next generation of these vessels may benefit from the incorporation of a high-speed, shallow-draft, large-flight-deck design that has the capability to send amphibious triage teams ashore.

Advancements in vertical takeoff and landing (VTOL) aircraft offer additional opportunities towards the improvement of medical evacuation and logistics as well. All of the services have recognized the incredible potential of tilt-rotor aircraft. The U.S. Marines, Navy, Air Force, and Special Operations Command have invested heavily in the V-22 Osprey program which saw service delivering medical supplies over 200 miles from Guantanamo Bay, Cuba during Operation Unified Response.[260] Had this capability been available during the emergency phase of the disaster in 2005, victims in Muzaffarabad could have hypothetically received medical support directly from to coalition hospitals in Afghanistan. While the V-22 doubles the capability of the UH-60 Blackhawk, the DoD's MEDEVAC proponent at Fort Rucker has not yet bought in to it.[261] As a part of the Future Vertical Lift Program, the U.S. Army is investing a third generation tilt-rotor aircraft known as the V-280 Valor. If delivered as promised, this

---

[258]The *USNS Comfort* and *Mercy* are now a part of the PACOM and SOUTHCOM Commander's 2013 health engagement strategies through "Pacific Partnership" and "Continuing Promise".

[259]Leah Averitt, "Chinese Hospital Ships and Soft Power," *Semaphore* no. 3, (April 2011): 1-2.

[260]U.S. Department of the Navy, *V-22 Osprey Guidebook 2011/*2012, U.S. Naval Air Systems Command, NAVAIR PMA-275 (Washington D.C.: Government Printing Office, 2012).

[261]The V-22's combat radius is 325 nautical miles at a cruising speed of 262 knots, the UH-60 is 121 nautical miles at 130 knots.

airframe will have the ability to project out to 800 nautical miles at 280 knots.[262] In 2004, such a capability could have dispatched assessment teams from the joint task-force headquarters near Bangkok, Thailand directly to relief sites in Banda Aceh, Indonesia within 2½ hours without stopping for fuel along the way. Regardless of the platform chosen, the emerging capabilities within VTOL aircraft shows potential for knocking down domain interface challenges. The reduction of these challenges reinforces the logic behind joint-medical integration.

Conclusion

The last 20-years have demonstrated that the DoD has both embraced and improved the effectiveness of MHS in FDR environments as voiced through its policy and doctrine. This monograph has shown that military health systems have moderately improved their capability of employing effective health service support capabilities to foreign disaster areas, however room for improvement still exists. Through this evolution, we can infer changes to the way that the DoD trains, organizes, and equips in order to meet the challenge of providing ready, relevant, responsive, and reliable medical capabilities in support of national security priorities. If the DoD's post-Cold War global shaping engagement strategy continues, the applicability of MHS in FDR is likely to grow.

As the DoD enters a period of austerity, it is important to remember the effect that these capabilities have provided.[263] Throughout the world, hundreds of thousands of lives have been saved or improved through the emergency care that was provided by a United States Soldier,

---

[262]Bell Helicopter News Release, "Army Awards JMR-TD Program Technology Investment Agreement With Bell Helicopter for Next-Generation Tiltrotor Demonstrator," Bell Helicopter, http://www.bellhelicopter.com/en_US/News/PressReleases/NewsRelease/NewsRelease.html?ReleaseID=1862643 (accessed 25 October, 2013).

[263]U.S. Department of Defense, *Defense Budget Priorities and Choices; Fiscal Year 2014* (Washington, D.C.: Government Printing Office, 2011), 1.

Sailor, or Airman. Every time affected parents remember that day that disaster came, they will think of those medics saving their child's life, limbs, or eyesight. Every time the world sees United States forces promptly arrive to an emergency, they will be reassured of America's commitment towards projecting capability and providing stability. Every time that the American people see their military pioneering the way into hell on missions of mercy, they will be able to be proud of what their country stands for. The physical and moral return on this investment is incredible.

BIBLIOGRAPHY

Abbasi, Mohammad-Ali et al., "Lessons Learned in Using Social Media for Disaster Relief." Paper presented at the International Conference on Social Computing, Behavioral-Cultural Modeling, and Prediction, College Park, MD, April 3-5, 2012.

Allard, Kenneth. *Somalia Operations: Lessons Learned.* Washington D.C.: National Defense University Press, 1995.

Averitt, Leah. "Chinese Hospital Ships and Soft Power." *Semaphore,* no. 3 (2011): 1-2.

Bell Helicopter News Release. "Army Awards JMR-TD Program Technology Investment Agreement With Bell Helicopter for Next-Generation Tiltrotor Demonstrator." Bell Helicopter, http://www.bellhelicopter.com/en_US/News/PressReleases/NewsRelease/NewsRelease.html?ReleaseID=1862643 (accessed 25 October, 2013).

Bessler, John. "Defining Criteria for Handover to Civilian Officials in Relief Operations" Master's thesis, U.S. Army War College, 2008.

Burkett, Edwin. "Foreign Sector Capacity Building and the U.S. Military." *Military Medicine* 177, no. 3 (2012): 298.

Burkett, Edwin and Jerry Tuero. "Developing Future Command Surgeons and Staff for Joint Operations Assignments." *Joint Center for Operational Analysis Journal* 12, no. 2 (2010): 51-54.

Carlson, Joel. "USS Carl Vinson's Medical Department Provides First Responder Care in Haiti." *Navy Medicine* 102, no 2 (2010): 12.

Crain, Nathaniel. "Haiti: Two Decades of Intervention and Very Little to Show." Monograph, Command and General Staff College, 2012.

Davis, Lois M. et al. *Army Medical Support for Peace Operations and Humanitarian Assistance.* Santa Monica, CA: RAND Corporation, 1996.

Dickson, Hendrick. "Navy Medicine Joins International Team at Haitian Field Hospital." *Navy Medicine* 102, no 2 (2010): 25-26.

Donohue, Tim. "Navy Medicine Hits the Blogosphere." *Navy Medicine* 102, no 2 (2010): 30.

Dubois, Laurent. *Haiti: The Aftershocks of History.* New York, NY: Metropolitan Books, 2012.

Ellman, Bruce. *Waves of Hope: The U.S. Navy's Response to the Tsunami in Northern Indonesia* Monograph, U.S. Naval War College, 2007.

Flynn, Charles and Joshua Richardson. "Joint Operational Access and the Global Response Force: Redefining Readiness." *Military Review* XCIII, no. 4 (2013): 42.

Hancock, Michele. "Medical Response to Haiti Earthquake: Operation Unified Response." Lecture, 2011 Military Health System Conference, National Harbor, MD, January 24, 2011.

Hanes, Sharon and Richard Hanes. *Cold War Primary Sources.* Farmington Hills, MI: UXL, 2004.

Hatch, Mary Jo. *Organization Theory: Modern, Symbolic, and Postmodern Perspectives.* 2nd ed. New York: Oxford University Press, 2006.

Hosek, Susan and Gary Cecchine. *Reorganizing the Military Health System: Should there be a Joint Command.* Santa Monica, CA: Rand National Security Research Division, MR-1350-OSD, 2001.

Joint Center for Operational Analysis. "Operation Unified Response: Haiti Earthquake Response." After action review presentation, Norfolk, VA, May 15, 2010.

Juatai, Joaquin. "*USS Abraham Lincoln* Medical Teams Provide Support in Banda Aceh." *Navy Medicine* 96, no. 2 (2005): 10-13.

Kaiser, Reinhard et al. "The Application of Geographic Information Systems and Global Positioning Systems in Humanitarian Emergencies: Lessons Learned, Programme Implications, and Future Research." *Disasters* 27, no. 2 (2003): 127-140.

Keen, Ken et al. "Foreign Disaster Response: Joint Task Force Haiti Observations." *Military Review* 90, no. 6 (2010): 85.

Kretchik Walter E., Robert F. Baumann, and John T. Fishel, *Invasion, Intervention, "Intervasion": A Concise History of the U.S. Army in Operation Uphold Democracy.* Fort Leavenworth, KS: Command and General Staff College Press, 1998.

Kuhn, Thomas S. *The Structure of Scientific Revolutions.* 3rd. ed. Chicago: The University of Chicago Press, 1996.

Lefebvre, Paule. *"Operation Unified Assistance."* Presentation given at the National Defense University 2005 Pacific Symposium, Waikiki, HI, June 10, 2005.

Licina, Derek. "Hospital Ships Adrift: A Systematic Literature Review Characterizing US Navy Hospital Ship Humanitarian and Disaster Response." *Prehospital and Disaster Medicine* 28, no. 3 (July 2013): 1-9.

Lieven, Anatol *Pakistan: A Hard Country.* New York: Public Affairs, 2011.

Metz, Helen Chapin. ed. *Somalia: A Country Study,* 4th ed. Washington D.C: Government Printing Office, 1993.

Mendel, William W. "The Haiti Contingency." *Military Review* (January 1994): 49-50.

Miller, James. "Public Diplomacy and Foreign Disaster Relief: Machiavellian or Altruistic Approach?" Research paper, U.S. Army War College, 2011.

Military Factory. "USNS Comfort (T-AH-20) Medical Support Vessel." http://www.militaryfactory.com/ships/detail.asp?ship_id=USNS-Comfort-TAH20 (accessed October 5, 2013).

Morgan, Gareth. *Images of Organization.* Thousand Oaks, CA: Sage Publications, 2006.

Mosier William A. and Walter H. Orthner. "Military Medical Support for Humanitarian Assistance and Disaster Relief: Lessons Learned From the Pakistan Earthquake Relief Effort." *Joint Center for Operational Analysis* 9, no. 2 (June 2007): 7.

Munsey, Christopher. "Navy medicine moves closer to combat zone – Hospital ships likely to retire, surgical teams head ashore in new plan to treat wounded." *Navy Times*, August 9, 2004.

NATO. *The Haiti Case Study.* Joint Analysis and Lessons Learned Centre, Lisbon, 2012.

The National Research Council. *The U.S. Government Foreign Disaster Assistance Program.* Washington, D.C.: National Academy of Sciences, 1978.

Rabasa, Angel and Peter Chalk. *Indonesia's Transformation and the Stability of Southeast Asia.* Santa Monica, CA: RAND, 2001.

Rencoret, Nicole et al. *Haiti Earthquake Response: Context Analysis.* London: Active Learning Network for Accountability and Performance in Humanitarian Action Secretariat (July 2010): 9.

Robinson, Adam. "Navy Medicine Supports Earthquake Relief." *Navy Medicine* 102, no 2 (2010): 4.

Schaffer, Teresita. *Kashmir: The Economics of Peace Building.* Washington D.C.: Center for Strategic and International Studies, 2005.

Schmidt, John. *The Unraveling: Pakistan in the Age of Jihad.* New York: Picador, 2011.

Schon, Donald. *Educating the Reflective Practitioner.* San Francisco: Jossey-Bass, 1987.

Shaw, Christina. "Bataan Medical Team Supports Haiti Relief." *Navy Medicine* 102, no 2 (2010): 22-24.

Clarke, Walter S. *Somalia: Background Information for Operation Restore Hope.* Carlisle Barracks: U.S. Army War College, 1992.

Shirly, Eric. "Joint Aeromedical Evacuation: Why Isn't it Adequate for the Combat Zone?" Master's thesis, Naval War College, 2004.

Smith, Michael. "A Better Disaster Response: Building a Solid Foundation." Monograph, Naval War College, 2009.

Surette, Cappy. "Navy and Civilian Medical Teams Work Together to Provide Hope on Comfort." *Navy Medicine* 102, no 2 (2010): 20.

Thompson, Wiley. "Perfect Strangers: An Examination of Contemporary Military Involvement in Humanitarian Affairs." *Journal of Military Geography* Special Edition 1 (2010): 4.

Warner, Shannon. "USNS Comfort Crew Holds Ceremony for Haitians." *Navy Medicine* 102, no 2 (2010).

The White House. *National Security Strategy*. Washington, D.C.: White House, 2010.

U.S. Department of the Air Force. *Air Mobility Planning Factors*. Air Force Pamphlet 10-1403. Washington D.C.: Government Printing Office (2003): 10.

U.S. Department of the Air Force. *Health Services*. Air Force Doctrine Document 2-4.2. Washington, D.C.: Government Printing Office, 1999.

U.S. Department of the Air Force. *Medical Operations*. Air Force Doctrine Document 4-02. Washington, D.C.: Government Printing Office (2012): 29-32.

U.S. Department of the Air Force. *Operations Other Than War*. Air Force Doctrine Document 2-3. Washington, D.C.: Government Printing Office (1996): 12.

U.S. Department of the Air Force. *With Compassion and Hope: The Story of Operation Unified Assistance*. Hickam Air Force Base, HI: Headquarters, Pacific Air Forces Office of History (2006): 18-22.

U.S. Department of the Army. *Army Health System* ATTP 4-02. Washington, D.C.: Government Printing Office, 2011.

U.S. Department of the Army. *Army Health System* ATTP 4-02. Washington, D.C.: Government Printing Office, 2013.

U.S. Department of the Army. *Army Health System* FM 4-02. Washington, D.C.: Government Printing Office, 2013.

U.S. Department of the Army. *Casualty Care* ATP 4-02.5. Washington, D.C.: Government Printing Office, 2013.

U.S. Department of the Army. *Force Health Protection in a Global Environment* FM 4-02. Washington, D.C.: Government Printing Office, 2003.

U.S. Department of the Army. *Medical Evacuation* FM 4-02.2. Washington, D.C.: Government Printing Office, 2011.

U.S. Department of the Army. *Medical Support Theater of Operations* FM 8-10. Washington D.C.: Government Printing Office, 1970.

U.S. Department of the Army. *Multi-Service Techniques for Civil Affairs Support to Foreign Humanitarian Assistance* ATP 3-57.20. Washington, D.C.: Government Printing Office, 2013.

U.S. Department of the Army. *Operations* FM 100-5. Washington, D.C.: Government Printing Office, 1993.

U.S. Department of the Army. *Planning for Health Service Support* FM 8-55. Washington, D.C.: Government Printing Office, 1994.

U.S. Department of the Army. *Stability* ADP 3-07. Washington, D.C.: Government Printing Office, 2012.

U.S. Department of the Army. *Sustainment,* ADP 4-0. Washington, D.C.: Government Printing Office, 2012.

U.S. Department of the Army. *United States Forces After Action Review and Historical Overview: The United States Army in Somalia.* Washington D.C.: Center of Military History (2003): 201.

U.S. Department of the Army. *Army Health System* FM 4-02. Washington, D.C.: Government Printing Office, 2013.

U.S. Department of the Army. "The United States Army in Somalia: 1992-1994." Department of Military History, http://www.history.army.mil/brochures/Somalia/Somalia.htm (downloaded 10 October, 2008).

U.S. Department of the Army. *Combat Health Support in Stability Operations and Support Operations* FM 8-42. Washington, D.C.: Government Printing Office, 1997.

U.S. Department of the Army. *Operations* FM 3-0. Washington D.C.: Government Printing Office, 2000.

U.S. Department of the Defense. *Doctrine for the Armed Forces of the United States* JP 1. Washington, D.C.: Government Printing Office, 2013.

U.S. Department of Defense. *Department of Defense Support to Foreign Disaster Relief* GTA 90-01-030. Washington D.C.: Government Printing Office, 2011.

U.S. Department of Defense. *Foreign Humanitarian Assistance* JP 3-29. Washington, D.C.: Government Printing Office, 2009.

U.S. Department of Defense. *Health Service Support* JP 4-02. Washington, D.C.: Government Printing Office, 2012.

U.S. Department of Defense. *Doctrine for Health Service Support in Joint Operations* JP 4-02. Washington, D.C.: Government Printing Office, 1994.

U.S. Department of Defense. *Doctrine for Health Service Support in Joint Operations* JP 4-02. Washington, D.C.: Government Printing Office, 2001.

U.S. Department of the Navy. *Humanitarian Assistance/Disaster Relief Operations Planning* NWDC TACMEMO 3-07.6-05. Washington, D.C.: Government Printing Office, 2005.

U.S. Department of Defense. *Joint Tactics, Techniques, and Procedures for Foreign Humanitarian Assistance* JP 3-07.6. Washington, D.C.: Government Printing Office, 2001.

U.S. Department of Defense. *Military Health Support for Stability Operations.* Department of Defense Instruction 6000.16, 2010.

U.S. Department of Defense. *Stability Operations.* Department of Defense Directive 3000.05, 2005.

U.S. Department of Defense. *Stability Operations.* Department of Defense Instruction 3000.05, 2009.

U.S. Department of Defense. *Defense Budget Priorities and Choices, Fiscal Year 2014.* Washington, D.C.: Government Printing Office, 2011.

U.S. Department of Defense. *Department of Defense Support to Foreign Disaster Relief: Handbook for JTF Commanders and Below* GTA 90-01-030. Washington, D.C.: Government Printing Office, 2011.

U.S. Department of Defense. *Responsibility for Foreign Disaster Relief Operations.* Department of Defense Directive 5100.46, 1964.

U.S. Department of Defense. *Foreign Humanitarian Assistance* JP 3-29. Washington, D.C.: Government Printing Office, 2009.

U.S. Department of Defense. *Task Force on Military Health System Governance Final Report.* Washington, D.C., 2011.

U.S. Department of Defense. *Doctrine for Joint Operations* JP 3-0. (Washington, D.C.: Government Printing Office, 1993.

U.S. Department of Defense. *Doctrine for Health Service Support in Joint Operations* JP 4-02. Washington, D.C.: Government Printing Office, 1995.

U.S. Department of Defense. "Fiscal Year 2013 Budget Estimates, Defense Security Cooperation Agency, February 2013." http://comptroller.defense.gov/defbudget/fy2013/budget_justification/pdfs/01_Operation_and_Maintenance/O_M_VOL_1_PARTS/O_M_VOL_1_BASE_PARTS/OHDACA_OP-5.pdf (accessed August 30, 2013)

U.S. Department of Defense. *Joint Doctrine for Military Operations Other Than War* JP 3-07. Washington, D.C.: Government Printing Office, 1995.

U.S. Department of Defense. *Multiservice Procedures for Humanitarian Assistance Operations* FM 100-23-1. Washington, D.C.: Government Printing Office, 1994.

U.S. Department of Health and Human Services. *National Disaster Medical System Federal Coordination Center Guide.* Washington, D.C., 2010.

U.S. Department of the Navy. *Humanitarian Assistance/Disaster Relief Operations Planning* TM 3-07.6-05. Washington, D.C.: Government Printing Office, 1996.

U.S. Department of the Navy. *Naval Humanitarian Assistance Missions* EXTAC 1011. Washington, D.C.: Government Printing Office, 2005.

U.S. Department of the Navy. *V-22 Osprey Guidebook 2011/2012 U.S. Naval Air Systems Command* NAVAIR PMA-275. Washington D.C.: Government Printing Office, 2012.

U.S. Department of the Navy. *Humanitarian Assistance/Disaster Relief Operations Planning,* NWDC TACMEMO 3-07.6-05. Washington D.C.: Government Printing Office, 2005.

U.S. Government Accountability Office. *Report to the Chairman, Subcommittee on National Security and Foreign Affairs, Committee on Oversight and Government Reform, House of Representatives.* GAO Document 10-801. Washington, D.C., 2010.

Whitcomb, Darrel. *Call Sign-Dustoff: A History of U.S. Army Aeromedical Evacuation from Conception to Katrina.* Fort Detrick, MD: Office of the Surgeon General, 2011.

Wiharta, Sharon et al. *The Effectiveness of Foreign Military Assets in Natural Disaster Response.* Solna, Sweden: The Stockholm International Peace Research Institute, 2008.

Woodhead, Amanda. "USNH Okinawa Sends Medical Relief and Supplies to Southeast Asia." *Navy Medicine* 96, no.2 (2005).